D1385226

Household Composition and Racial Inequality

Household Composition and Racial Inequality

Suzanne M. Bianchi

Rutgers University Press / *New Brunswick*

Library of Congress Cataloging in Publication Data

Bianchi, Suzanne M
  Household composition and racial inequality.

  Bibliography: p.
  Includes index.
    1. Family—United States—Statistics.   2. Afro-
American families—Statistics.   3. Single-parent
family—United States—Statistics.   4. Households
—United States—Statistics.   5. Income distribu-
tion—United States—Statistics.   6. Family size—
Economic aspects—United States—Statistics.
I. Title.
HQ536.B5   306.8   80-39761
ISBN 0–8135–0913–0

To Mac

Contents

List of Figures

List of Tables

Acknowledgments

This volume is a revision of my doctoral dissertation, which was completed in 1978 while I was at the Population Studies Center of the University of Michigan. My greatest debt is to the members of my dissertation committee, in particular Reynolds Farley. Ren suggested the topic to me initially, chaired the dissertation committee, and served as a sounding board throughout the writing and rewriting of the manuscript. The insights and suggestions of the other members of the committee, Deborah Freedman, Al Hermalin, and Karen Mason, are gratefully acknowledged.

Financial assistance was provided by the Employment and Training Administration of the U.S. Department of Labor, Grant No. 91–26–78–24. A small Ford Foundation Research Grant, awarded by the Center for Continuing Education of Women at the University of Michigan, was also instrumental in the early stages of the analysis. Invaluable computer programming assistance was provided by J. Michael Coble and Karlin Richardson. Carol Crawford typed the original manuscript and Terry Milton assisted in typing the revision.

A version of Chapter 6 appeared in the May 1980 issue of *Demography* under the title, "Racial Differences in Per Capita Income 1960–76: The Importance of Household Size, Headship and Labor Force Participation." Helpful comments on that paper were provided by Gordon Green, Larry Suter, Linda Waite, James Wetzel and two anonymous reviewers.

Frances Kobrin, in reviewing the manuscript for publication, provided extremely useful suggestions for the revision of

Chapter 3. The comments of the other reviewer pointed out several necessary changes to the original manuscript.

Finally, the encouragement and editorial assistance of Marlie Wasserman and Leslie Mitchner of Rutgers University Press are most appreciated.

Household Composition and Racial Inequality

Chapter 1

Introduction

Since the passage of the Equal Pay Act of 1963 and the Civil Rights Act of 1964, a series of legislative and executive acts have been aimed at guaranteeing equal access to educational and employment opportunities for all individuals regardless of race or sex. Not surprisingly, the majority of studies of racial inequality have focused on the educational, occupational, and earnings attainment of black and white individuals. Generally, the findings lead to the conclusion that socioeconomic improvements in the lives of black individuals were greater in the prosperous 1960s but did not disappear in the recessionary 1970s (Farley, 1977, 1979).

The picture for families is somewhat different. Median family income for blacks increased substantially in the 1960s, but the position of black families relative to white families seems to have deteriorated in the 1970s. A significant factor has been the greater increase among blacks in the proportion of families that are female-headed, that is, families likely to have low incomes (Farley, 1977; Treas and Walther, 1978; Slater, 1980; Green and Welniak, 1980).

In the United States in recent decades, household and family living arrangements have changed dramatically among both blacks and whites. Young adults and older people are increasingly likely to live alone or with nonrelatives rather than to reside with family members. Sharp increases in divorce and in births out-of-wedlock have resulted in a growing number of children spending at least part of their childhood in households in which one parent, usually the father, is absent. Among both blacks and whites, there has been a decline in the proportion of men, women, and children who at any given point are found living in traditional husband–wife families. Even within households headed by a married couple, important changes in the economic and familial roles of women have occurred as fertility within marriage declines and more wives enter the labor force.

Research that focuses on individual employment and earnings inequality, while important in its own right, does not provide a comprehensive assessment of the economic well-being of blacks vis-à-vis whites. Households or families operate as the basic unit for pooling and sharing individual resources, and among households, individuals support varying numbers of dependents. If the goal of research is to assess the relative well-being of all segments of the population, studies must also take into account racial differences in living arrangements and changes over time in household composition.

This analysis is motivated by the idea that we may be at the intersection of two major trends—each working counter to the other. On the one hand, the legislation that has grown out of the civil rights movement, the war on poverty, and the women's movement represents a serious public commitment to eliminate racial and sexual discrimination in schooling, jobs, and wages. On the other hand, substantial changes in family living arrangements have occurred and what transpires within families and within and between households remains largely outside of the realm of governmental policy. It is conceivable (and indeed there is some evidence) that shifts in living arrangements and family structure may be attenuating the effect of measures designed to improve the opportunities of blacks and women—measures designed ultimately to improve the economic well-being of all individuals, dependents as well as earners.[1] The shifts are, at minimum, complicating the flow of income between parents and their children. A major unanswered question is how much of the racial difference in economic well-being is due to differences in household size and structure and how much is due to different employment patterns and sources of income.

Any study that considers racial differences in living arrangements as explicit components in racial differences in economic status will no doubt be linked to the oft-cited report by Daniel Moynihan, *The Negro Family: The Case for National Action* (1965). Moynihan's thesis, that the deterioration of black families is the fundamental source of weakness in the black community, evoked a great deal of controversy and criticism within the academic community (see Rainwater and Yancey, 1967), although it generated little in the way of social policy.

The present work is more tolerant of the existence of family forms other than nuclear husband–wife families than the Moynihan report was. It is not based on the idea that black families must be "strengthened" and made to look more like white families, but it does point out that single parents raising dependent children encounter serious economic difficulties. Although the focus of my analysis is on racial differences in economic welfare, this book is as much about sex inequality as it is racial inequality. And, insofar as it is a study of changes in family structure, it is a study of changes among whites as well as among blacks.

As with the Moynihan report, the present work seeks to provide insight into effective strategies for eliminating racial inequalities in economic well-being, inequalities that truly remain a "case for national action." The underlying assumption is that living arrangements and economic relationships are so intertwined that the two must be considered in conjunction if reasonable social policy is to be formulated.

The scope of social indicators considered in this analysis is less broad than in the Moynihan report, but the analysis is more thorough and systematic. Two measures of economic well-being that adjust for differences in household size (need levels) are constructed and used to assess the trend in racial inequality for the 1960–1976 period. One measure is similar to Morgan's (1974a) "income/needs" measure and is referred to as a household's welfare ratio. The other is a per capita income measure. After describing the unit of analysis and data in Chapter 2, I discuss the construction of the measures of well-being in detail.

Racial inequality in well-being is a function of differences in both household income and household financial needs. That is, well-being in black households is lower than in white households because income is lower in black households on average and because need levels are higher. Changes in living arrangements of blacks and whites, which have been substantial during the last two decades, affect both components of well-being. Chapter 3 is devoted to describing changes in household size and composition of blacks and whites since the late 1950s.

In Chapter 4, my discussion turns to sources of income in black and white households. Total income differences are disaggregated into differences in earnings and other sources of income. Because earnings form a major component of income in most families, a large portion of Chapter 4 is devoted to a systematic breakdown of earnings in black and white households. Specifically, I describe racial differences and changes over time in the proportion of households that have earnings from husbands or other male heads, wives or other female heads, and other adults; the extent of labor market participation (i.e., the average annual hours of labor market activity) of these types of earners; and the average annual earnings they contributed to a household.

The labor force activity and earnings of nonelderly husbands, wives, and other male and female heads are investigated in detail in Chapter 5 because the earnings of these individuals are of primary importance to their respective households. Regression standardization is used to decompose racial differences and changes over time in earnings into what is attributable to, on the one hand, compositional differences between groups in marital–family status, education, occupation, and experience, and on the other hand, to differences in dollar returns to similar labor market characteristics.

In Chapter 6, overall changes in racial inequality in economic well-being are evaluated using the measures constructed in Chapter 2. After assessing the 1960–1970 and 1970–1976 trends in well-being of blacks and whites, the racial gap is broken down into a household type component and a "pure" income component. Within similar types of households, per capita income differences are decomposed into household size and income components. Improvement over time in per capita income within black and white households is also apportioned to both the decline in household size and the growth in real income. The relative importance of earnings versus other income improvements for different types of households, as well as the significance of changes in employment, annual hours worked, and implicit wage rates of household heads are estimated.

In my concluding chapter, 7, I discuss some of the economic causes and consequences of 1960–1976 changes in living arrangements and their implications for family policy.

Chapter 2

Defining the Household and Measuring Economic Well-Being

My analysis relies upon the one-in-one-thousand public use samples of the 1960 and 1970 censuses of population and the March 1976 Annual Demographic Microdata File of the Current Population Survey (CPS). These samples provide a representative cross-section of U.S. households at each point in time. The family relationships of household members are coded, but because the sampling unit is the household, families include only those persons related by blood, marriage, or adoption, *who reside together in the same household unit*. As I will discuss in Chapter 3, there has been a substantial increase over this 16-year period in the number of persons who live alone or with nonrelatives. Residence with family members encompasses a smaller portion of a person's life cycle than in the past. If my assessment of black–white differences in economic well-being were restricted to families, a significant and growing share of both the black and white population would be eliminated from this study.

Hence, I chose the household, and not the more restricted family unit as a basis for analysis, and when individuals are considered, it is with explicit regard for their status as members of a particular household. The vast majority of persons in the United States—black and white—reside in households, the living arrangements of which define important income pooling arrangements. Whereas the pooling assumption underlying this analysis is perhaps more tenuous for unrelated individuals than for family members, people do not have to be related to share costs or to benefit from economies of scale associated with living in larger units. Living in the same house or apartment facilitates (and often necessitates) the sharing of physical space and the sharing of resources such as time and money. To the extent that household living arrangements are voluntary, "deciding whether or not to live together requires considering desires for independence and dependency, and for privacy and companionship which are important factors in any relationship" (Kobrin, 1976:137).

Ideally, an assessment of economic well-being should take into account the sharing and transferring of money, goods, and services both within and between households. Limitations of the data restrict my analysis to sharing of monetary income within households. Census and CPS data, however, do allow one to build a fairly complete picture of a household's income and financial needs. Data have been collected on all individuals residing in a housing unit and each individual can be linked to the others in the same household. Information about the age, sex, race, family status, and relationship to the head is available for all household members. For persons 14 years old and over, additional information is available on employment status, hours worked in the week preceding the census survey, weeks worked, income from earnings and other sources in the year preceding the survey, years of school completed, occupation, and marital status.

The samples are large enough that racial comparisons can be made with a high degree of reliability and household types that are a small proportion of all households can be analyzed. A comprehensive picture of relative well-being in the United States and racial inequality in that respect requires as detailed a picture of different household types as possible. This is the major reason for using census and CPS data rather than some other data source such as the Panel Study of Income Dynamics. My analysis is based on approximately 47,000 white households and 4,700 black households in 1960; 58,000 white and 6,000 black households in 1970; and 40,000 white and 4,700 black households in 1976.

Comparability of census and CPS data is quite high.[1] Concepts and question wording are similar, usually identical. All data have been collected by the U.S. Bureau of the Census so there is continuity in the data collection and data management procedures. There are some differences in the variables contained on the census and CPS data files. For instance, the census public use tapes contain a variable indicating rural or urban residence but the CPS annual demographic file does not. The CPS file contains more detailed breakdowns of income from sources other than earnings. Also, more labor force information is available on the CPS file.

Measures used in this analysis are comparable across the three data sources. Procedures for constructing new or composite variables are the same for both races and for each time point and therefore facilitate racial comparisons and the study of time trends.

Household Headship

The census and CPS data files are such that for each household one person is designated as "head."[2]

The head of the household is usually the person regarded as the head by members of the household. Women are not classified as heads if their husbands are resident members of the household at the time of the survey. Married couples related to the head of a household are included in the head's household and are not classified as separate households (U.S. Bureau of the Census, 1977a:16).

In this analysis, the proportion of black and white households in which the designated head was neither the main earner nor the main income recipient was ascertained. In only about 6 percent of white households and 7 percent of black households was the designated head not the economic dominant within the household.

The data records for one hundred of the households in which the economic dominant was someone other than the head were scrutinized. About half of these cases were ones in which the designated head was a male whose wife was actually the more important income source. In most other households, even though the designated head was not the main earner, the designation either seemed appropriate or it was unclear who else should be considered household head. For example, most of these were households in which either no one earned much and the designated head was a parent under 65 living with children, or a parent was earning a reasonable income but a young adult son or daughter was earning a larger amount, or a non-earning female head under 60 was living with her children and one of the children was the main wage earner. Since parents who are not elderly might be assumed to have some authority over, and obligations to, children living with them, even adult wage-earning children, it seemed reasonable to leave these designations as they were.

In households in which there seemed no clear rationale for choosing any person as head (i.e., households in which all persons were unrelated and the person designated as head was not the main earner or did not appear to have some other economically dominant position in the household such as owning the home), the labor activities of the chief income recipient are analyzed in detail and this person is treated as the household head for classification purposes.

Finally, in households labeled "husband–wife," the wife's labor activities, as well as the husband's, are analyzed in detail. The husband is not automatically considered household head. Rather, these households might be considered to have two heads, or co-heads.

Table 2.1. Number of Sample Households by Race and
Type of Head

	1960 n	1970 n	1976 n
White			
Total households	47,112	55,769	40,378
Total husband–wife			
head	35,733	39,324	27,011
With children <18	21,682	22,233	14,379
Without children	14,051	17,091	12,632
Total female head	7,769	11,200	9,120
Living alone	4,085	6,464	5,398
With nonrelatives	433	535	376
With relatives,			
no children	1,607	1,814	1,243
With relatives,			
children	1,644	2,387	2,103
Total male head	3,610	5,245	4,247
Living alone	2,196	3,367	2,877
With nonrelatives	277	570	635
With relatives,			
no children	802	791	470
With relatives,			
children	335	517	265

Description of the Sample

Analysis is restricted to households headed by a black or white individual who was not a member of the armed forces at the time of the census survey. Table 2.1 shows the number of black and white sample households—classified as either black or white on the basis of the race of the household head—upon which estimates are based.[3] In Table 2.1 households are divided into those headed by a husband and wife, those headed by a female, and those headed by a male. Husband–wife house-

Table 2.1, continued

	1960 n	1970 n	1976 n
Black			
Total households	4,723	6,145	4,717
Total husband–wife			
head	2,881	3,180	2,078
With children <18	1,898	2,068	1,312
Without children	983	1,112	766
Total female head	1,317	2,129	1,919
Living alone	409	679	621
With nonrelatives	76	70	55
With relatives,			
no children	232	272	218
With relatives,			
children	600	1,108	1,025
Total male head	525	836	720
Living alone	302	511	477
With nonrelatives	73	86	101
With relatives,			
no children	80	94	76
With relatives,			
children	70	145	66

holds are further divided into those with and without dependent children (i.e., children < 18). Female-headed households are divided into four categories: women living alone, with nonrelatives, with relatives and in households in which all members are adults (i.e., ≥ 18), and with relatives and in households in which some members are dependent children. The classification of male-headed households in Table 2.1 is like that of female-headed households.

Table 2.2 presents the total numbers of individuals living in black and white husband–wife, female-headed, and male-

Table 2.2. Number of Individuals Living in Sample Households

	1960		1970		1976	
	n	%	n	%	n	%
White						
Total individuals	152,560	100.0	170,009	100.0	114,870	100.0
husband–wife head	131,582	86.2	140,882	82.9	92,464	80.5
female head	14,905	9.8	20,508	12.1	16,114	14.0
male head	6,073	4.0	8,619	5.0	6,292	5.5
Black						
Total individuals	18,139	100.0	21,779	100.0	14,947	100.0
husband–wife head	13,046	71.9	13,760	63.2	8,286	55.4
female head	4,060	22.4	6,446	29.6	5,513	36.9
male head	1,033	5.7	1,573	7.2	1,148	7.7

headed sample households at each of the three time points. As can be seen from the table, this analysis makes use of data on approximately 150,000 household members in white households and 18,000 in black households in 1960; 170,000 whites and 22,000 blacks in 1970; and 115,000 whites and 15,000 blacks in 1976.

Measuring Economic Well-Being

An ideal measure of the well-being of household members should include cultural, social, and psychological, as well as economic dimensions. Although attempts have been made to delineate social and psychological aspects of well-being, widespread agreement on these indicators does not exist. At least with respect to the economic dimension, there is some agreement as to what should be included in a measure of well-being. Several procedures for arriving at such a measure do exist, although each has its imperfections. Most often these economic measures, when they go beyond individual or household earnings or income, involve some algebraic manipulation of two components: household income and household economic need levels. For example, Morgan (1974a:13) in his analysis of data from *A Panel Study of Income Dynamics* (1972), most frequently uses an "income/needs ratio" that is the ratio of household money income to a money need standard similar to the official poverty thresholds used by the Bureau of the Census.

In constructing a well-being measure based on income and needs, one question that arises is what should be included in the determination of a household's income. This is particularly important for racial comparisons if inclusions (or exclusions) are biased in favor of one race or the other. Levitan, Johnston, and Taggart (1975) make the point that whites are more likely to have capital gains and profits and are more likely to own their homes than are blacks. On the other hand, there is evidence from the panel study that blacks are somewhat more likely than whites to receive public assistance income (Katherine Dickinson, 1974). In addition, some analysts have suggested that interfamily, interhousehold sharing may be more extensive among blacks (see Hill, 1977; Stack, 1974).

Exclusion of certain sources of income can also bias comparisons of well-being over time because these sources can become more (or less) important with time. Relevant examples for the present analysis are such public in-kind transfers as food stamps, rent subsidies, and school lunch programs. These have become increasingly important sources of income during the last decade and their exclusion represents a bias for more recent, as opposed to earlier, dates (see Smeeding, 1977; Plotnick and Skidmore, 1975).

The other important factor in the consideration of a well-being measure is the determination of household economic need. There is widespread consensus that family or household welfare and poverty measures should be adjusted in some way for differences in household size and composition (U.S. Department of Health, Education, and Welfare, 1976:I:25). The determination of a household need level involves some judgment as to what constitutes an adequate standard of living. In addition, one must determine which family compositional factors ought to enter into a calculation of needs. Finally, there is the further technical question: How does one go about assigning a dollar value to a household's level of need?

In my analysis, two measures of economic well-being are constructed and compared to household income. Changes in per capita income are presented for individual household members and total pretax, posttransfer household money income is related to a measure of household need incorporating adjustments for children's ages and economies of scale. In the following two sections of this chapter, I discuss the income and need measures in more detail.

Measuring Income / The census and Current Population Survey (CPS) collect data from all household members 14 years old and over on money income received in the preceding calendar year from wages or salary, income from farm and nonfarm self-employment, interest, dividends, rents, transfers such as Social Security, public assistance, veteran's payments, unemployment compensation, pensions, alimony and child support, and other regular and periodic money contributions from persons not living in the household (U.S. Bureau of the Census, 1977a:11).

Income tends to be underreported and the Bureau of the Census regularly compares its estimates with those from independent sources such as the Bureau of Economic Analysis and the Social Security Administration. It is estimated that income data collected in the March 1976 CPS were underreported by about 10 percent but there was wide variation by income source. Underreporting ranged from slightly under 60 percent for interest income and workman's compensation to only about 3 percent for wage and salary income, which comprise the largest income source in a majority of households (U.S. Bureau of the Census, 1977d:226).

Noncomparabilities exist in the data collection procedures among the two censuses and the CPS. Whereas the 1960 and 1970 censuses relied in part on self-enumeration, 1976 CPS data were obtained by a household interviewer. Although households were asked to report on the same sources of income in both censuses and the CPS, a much more detailed set of questions was used to probe for income other than earnings in the CPS than in either census. A comparison of 1970 census and 1970 CPS data indicates that household members are more likely to report that they received income from sources other than earnings in the CPS than in the census. This noncomparability would be particularly problematic for the 1970–1976 comparisons in the present analysis, except that reports of average amounts from other sources are higher in the census than in the CPS. The net result is that estimates of the proportion of household income from earnings and from other sources are very similar for the 1970 census and the 1970 CPS.

Although noncomparabilities between census and CPS data tend to balance out in the way I have described, and although underreporting of income is quite small for earnings (i.e., the major income source in most households), certain other omissions make census and CPS estimates less than ideal measures of the actual income that households have available for attending to member needs. An ideal measure would also include income from capital gains and the sale of property, adjust for federal and state income taxes, incorporate a valuation for in-kind transfers, such as food stamps, and assess the value of fringe benefits, such as insurance coverage. Household income might also be adjusted to include assets, such as equity in a home, although it should be noted that assets are less important for short-term expenditure capacity than are more liquid forms of income, such as earnings and cash transfers. The exclusion of taxes from data collected in the censuses and CPS biases upward welfare estimates, while the exclusion of assets, capital gains, in-kind transfers, and the underreporting of income biases downward estimates of well-being.

Smeeding (1977:161–165) has attempted to estimate income inequality and poverty for the 1968–1972 period by adjusting CPS income figures for the omission of taxes, the underreporting of income, and the omission of public in-kind transfers (i.e., food stamps, Medicare and Medicaid payments, and public housing subsidies). Based on his adjusted figures, he contends that there has been some narrowing of income inequality and substantially greater reductions in the incidence of poverty during the 1968–1972 period than appears in published census reports. That is, noncash transfers have increased in the last ten years and have become an important economic component of the well-being in low-income households. The exclusion of these transfers leads to an overestimate of the proportion of households and persons in poverty.

Smeeding's adjustments are carefully done, as far as they go. In drawing his conclusions about poverty and income inequality, however, he accepts uncritically official poverty thresholds and fails to mention some important omissions in the income data collected by the CPS, for which he does not correct—that is, private in-kind transfers such as perquisites that come with higher income jobs, the omission of capital gains, income from the sale of personal property, and assets such as home ownership. His findings are nonetheless suggestive and serve to emphasize the tentative nature of the trends and comparisons made using census and CPS data. Yet, even with these limitations, household income data collected by the census and the CPS are more complete and more accurate than those available from any other data source, except for perhaps the Panel Study of Income Dynamics.

Measuring Needs / Perhaps the most widely used estimates of the money income needs of families of various size and composition are those developed by Mollie Orshansky of the Social Security Administration (Orshansky, 1965). The Orshansky measure begins with food cost estimates for families of different size–age–sex structures. A multiplier is applied to the food budgets in order to estimate the total cost of a minimally adequate standard of living for a family of a given size with a given age–sex of head, a given number of adults, and a given number of children. Because fixed costs such as rent do not decline proportionally to food costs, an adjustment is made for the diseconomies of scale of one- and two-person households. An adjustment for rural or urban residence is also included. Thresholds are then adjusted annually for inflation by use of the Consumer Price Index.

Orshansky originally developed two sets of indicators: one based on the "economy" food plan and one on the higher "low cost" food plan of the U.S. Department of Agriculture (USDA). The lower of the two sets of estimates was adopted by the U.S. government and labeled the "official poverty thresholds." These remain the standards used by the U.S. Bureau of the Census in its annual estimates of the number of households and persons in poverty.[4]

In reviewing literature surrounding the adoption of the lower estimates, it is apparent that these became the official thresholds as much for their political acceptability and their availability at a time when a measure was needed as for their accuracy or adequacy (U.S. Department of Health, Education, and Welfare, 1976). Orshansky has noted that

at the Social Security Administration, we decided that we would develop two measures of need. . . . It was not the Social Security Administration that labeled the poverty line. It remained for the Office of Economic Opportunity and the Council of Economic Advisors to select the lower of the two measures and decide they would use it as a working tool. The best you can say for the measure is that at a time when it seemed useful, it was there. It is interesting that few outside the Social Security Administration ever wanted to talk about the higher measure. Everyone wanted only to talk about the lower one, labeled the "poverty line" . . . (1969:76).

In a similar vein, Plotnick and Skidmore concluded from their review that

the official thresholds, despite the particular derivation used to find them, simply reflect one rather stringent view of how much income is needed by different families to reach a minimum "level of decency" relative to average American standards. Their wide acceptance testifies only to their political acceptability and not to the intrinsic validity of the definition (1975:37).

Although Plotnick and Skidmore are critical of the standard, they use it in their work on poverty trends in the last decade and argue that this is justified because of the standard's wide acceptance and political–historical significance.

The major alternatives to the Orshansky procedures for determining household or family needs are measures—such as the Bureau of Labor Statistics' (BLS) Family Budget Costs—that estimate the cost of supporting a "typical" family of four and then use a set of equivalence scales to estimate the relative costs for different size families (U.S. Department of Health, Education, and Welfare, 1976). The assumption underlying the equivalence scales is that families spending an equal proportion of income on food have attained equivalent levels of living. The assumption makes BLS Family Budget Costs liable to some of the same criticisms leveled at the Orshansky poverty thresholds. (See the Appendix for more detail on the BLS procedures, critiques, and comparisons with the Orshansky poverty thresholds.)

For purposes of this analysis, it was necessary to arrive at a reasonable set of needs levels that could be fairly easily constructed for households of differing size and composition. Upon reviewing the relevant literature, it seemed apparent that the official poverty thresholds (i.e., the lower of the Orshansky estimates) were too low, especially since they would be used in conjunction with pretax income to arrive at a measure of well-being. Orshansky's procedures for arriving at a measure of needs (i.e., starting with food costs, then adjusting for other costs and for economies of scale), while in no sense absolute, were, however, reasonable. No clearly superior set of procedures has been developed.[5]

Procedures used to arrive at a needs measure for this analysis are similar to those used in arriving at the official thresholds, but with five modifications.

1. USDA food costs were used as a base and adjustments were made for other costs and for economies of scale. However, the higher "low cost" food budget estimates were used as a base rather than the lower "economy" food cost estimates.

2. Additional findings concerning the direct costs of children of various ages by Espenshade (1973) and Oppenheimer (1976) were incorporated to arrive at cost factors for children from age 0 to 5, 6 to 12, and 13 to 17. Sex differences in costs of children were eliminated.

3. Age–sex differentials in the cost or need levels of adults were eliminated. If one follows Orshansky's procedures, young adult males, because they have higher food costs (which are multiplied by a factor of three to arrive at total costs), are determined to have higher overall need levels than women or older males. While it is probably true that young adult men have higher food costs, women and the elderly may incur more in the way of other—such as medical—costs (Morgan, 1978; Moon, 1977). Thus, age–sex differentials were not considered justifiable.

4. Clair Vickery (1977) has noted the importance in determining household need levels of considering time available for housework and for child care. She notes that minimal nonpoor levels of consumption require both money and hours of household production. For example, official poverty standards are based on the assumption that all meals are prepared at home, and the BLS typical family has a nonworking wife.

Although there is no explicit assumption that a household with income equal to the poverty standard must have a person working full time in the home to be nonpoor, this assumption does seem to be implicit in the derivation of official poverty standards (Vickery, 1977:30).

Single adult households in which there are children and in which the adult is employed full time run a high risk of being "time poor" (Vickery, 1977:38). In some sense these households need additional income to buy services they cannot provide for themselves if they are to achieve minimally adequate living standards.

I used data from the ninth wave of the Panel Study of Income Dynamics conducted in 1976 to derive empirical estimates of the number of hours of housework and child care needed by households with differing numbers of adults and children of varying age levels. In any household in which there was a time shortage problem, the number of hours the household was short was valued at $4 an hour and this amount was added to the household's need level. The adjustment turned out to be fairly minor. Single adults had to have three or more children and be working full time before there was a time shortage and the shortage was not great unless all the children were young. The adjustment was included, however, because it seemed theoretically justifiable. (More detail is given in the Appendix.)

5. No adjustment for geographical location was included in the need calculations. Census data contain a variable indicating rural or urban residence but the CPS file does not. CPS data contain a variable indicating whether a household is located in one of the 35 largest Standard Metropolitan Statistical Areas (SMSA's) but the census contains nothing comparable to this. For 1976 a need measure with a regional SMSA adjustment was constructed and experimentally compared to the need figure that I use in this analysis. The regional adjustment made very little difference to the overall racial comparison (see the Appendix).

Briefly, the calculation of the household need measure used in my analysis was as follows. First, average estimates of food costs by age, based on 1967 USDA "low cost" food plans, were compiled for adults and age differences eliminated. Each individual 18 and over was estimated to need $7 a week in 1967, which is the USDA estimate of a young adult's food cost. Calculations of Espenshade (1973) and Oppenheimer (1976), in addition to USDA food budgets, by age, were used to arrive at ratios of the cost of children to adults. Weekly food costs were valued at $4 for those under 6, $5 for 6- to 11-year-olds, and $8 for teenagers. For each household, total annual food costs in 1967 dollars were determined by summing weekly costs of individual household members and multiplying this by 52. An economy of scale adjustment was introduced at this point: For single-person households, 20 percent was added to the food budget; 10 percent for two-person households; 5 percent for three-person households. For five-person households, 5 percent was subtracted, and for households of six or more, 10 percent was subtracted. These adjusted food budgets were multiplied by a factor of three to arrive at an estimate of total needs for food, clothing, housing, and other essentials. A multiplier of 3.7 was used for two-person households and 4.89 for single-person households since there are diseconomies of scale over and above those captured in the adjustment of food costs (e.g., disproportionately higher fixed costs in things like rent, utilities, etc.).[6] This total cost figure was then inflated by a factor of 1.612 (i.e., the ratio of the Consumer Price Index in 1975 to the base year 1967) to arrive at total costs in 1975 dollars.

A final adjustment for time shortages in some households was then made. That is, the 1976 Panel Study of Income Dynamics data, which contain indicators of the number of hours households spend on child care and housework, were used to estimate the number of housework hours required in households with 1, 2, or 3 or more adults, and 1, 2, 3, or 4 or more children ages 0–5, 6–13, and 14–17. Multiple classification analysis (MCA) was used to derive estimates. Table 2.3 presents results for selected households and the Appendix contains the complete MCA results. Every adult was assumed to need 11 hours a day for personal care, meals, and sleep—an estimate based on findings from time use studies (cf. Robinson, 1977). Each adult in

Table 2.3. Estimates of Housework and Child Care Hours

Household type	MCA results—Panel data	
	Annual	Weekly
1 adult with		
0 children	545	10
1 child	870–1,890[a]	17–36
2 children	1,200–2,500	23–49
3 children	1,400–3,100	28–59
2 adults with		
0 children	1636	31
1 child	2,000–3,000	38–57
2 children	2,300–3,600	44–70
3 children	2,500–4,200	49–80
Total sample (average)	1935	37.2

[a]Range is given. The value differs depending upon the age of the child (children).

the household was considered to have 4,745 hours per year left for market and nonmarket work and leisure. The number of annual hours each adult worked (i.e., the number of hours worked in the week prior to the census times the number of weeks worked last year) was subtracted from this figure to arrive at the maximum number of hours each adult in the household had available to do housework and care for children. Hours were summed over all adults and then the number of hours a particular household needed for child care and housework was subtracted from this figure. If there was an hours deficit, the number of hours a household was deficient was valued at $4 an hour—which was the average wage rate of service workers in 1975—and this was added to the total household need estimate.

Accuracy of Need Estimations / There are those who will argue that estimates using this particular need construction in relation to income understate well-being. Smeeding (1977) would probably suggest that even if a higher need threshold is more appropriate, the absence of an adjustment for in-kind transfers and underreporting of income leads to estimates of poverty here, as with official census reports, that are biased upward.

On the other hand, there are those who will consider these estimates still too low. Zimbalist (1977), for example, argues that a more appropriate need or poverty threshold would be about 50 percent higher than the official poverty thresholds. He arrives at this figure by arguing that not only are the food budgets that form the basis of the official thresholds too low—an argument accepted here and for which there has been a correction—but also that the multiplier of three used to arrive at total costs is too low. Lazear and Michael (1980) also suggest that a higher multiplier should be used, at least for one-person households.

As can be seen from Table 2.4, which compares this need construction to the official poverty thresholds used in census publications, a person living alone in 1975 is estimated to require around $3,500. This does not seem an unreasonably high figure, especially in a society with as high a standard of living as the United States. Estimates used in this analysis are generally higher than official thresholds, but distributions for total black and white households are quite comparable to those one would get if one used 125 percent the weighted average official poverty thresholds.

Alternate Measures of Well-Being

Changes in household composition, income, and members' labor force activity from 1960 to 1976 are reviewed in the following three chapters, leading up to my summary of the trend in well-being of blacks and whites in Chapter 6. One mea-

Table 2.4. Comparison of Household Need Measure with 1975 Official Poverty Thresholds for Selected Household Types

Household type	Official poverty threshold	Household need measure
1 person (male/female)	$2,902/2,685	$3,443
2 persons		
Husband–wife head	3,629	4,776
Female head, child 0–5	3,660	3,748
Female head, child 12–17	3,660	5,117
3 persons		
Female head, 2 children 0–5	4,307	3,961
Female head, 1 child 0–5, 1 child 6–11	4,307	4,488
Female head, 2 children 12–17	4,307	6,073
4 persons		
Husband–wife, 2 children 0–5	5,456	5,532
Husband–wife, 2 children 6–11	5,456	6,035
Husband–wife, 2 children 12–17	5,456	7,544

sure of well-being that I use is a household's welfare ratio—the ratio of household income to the household need measure just described.

Welfare ratios are easily thought of as household properties. The size of the measure is dependent on household size, composition, and time and money resources. Welfare ratios are presented for households, and averages for all blacks and whites represent averages weighted for the number of households.

Per capita income is also a function of household size, but such a measure apportions money resources equally to all unit members. Thus, it is easy to think of such a measure as being a property of individuals, and it provides an alternate view of the relative status of the total black and white population and change over time. Per capita income is presented for individuals, and averages for all blacks and whites represent averages weighted for the number of household members. That is, if per capita income is $2,000 in a six-person household and $3,500 in a one-person household, the average per capita income of those seven persons is $2,214, rather than $2,750, which would be the figure arrived at if per capita income figures were weighted by the number of households.

My goal is to assess accurately the progress that has been made in improving the living standards of blacks and whites. In presenting trends through alternate specifications of welfare measures, my intention is to strengthen the conclusions of this analysis. Comparisons of per capita and welfare ratio measures with household income can also suggest where trends are ambiguous.

Chapter 3

Changing Living Arrangements of Blacks and Whites

The manner in which persons group themselves, by choice or necessity, into household units is of great economic significance. Larger households generally have higher incomes than smaller ones but there are also more people sharing that income. Households with many dependents relative to earners will not be as well off financially as those with few or no dependents. If household living arrangements remain constant over time, they are not a very important consideration in assessing trends in income and earnings. Similarly, if the size and composition of black and white households were identical, living arrangements would not be particularly important to the study of racial differences in economic well-being.

The present chapter documents the fact that household living arrangements were anything but static during the 1960–1976 period. During the 1950s fertility was at high levels, divorce rates declined, and the American family went through a period of great stability. Beginning in the late 1950s, however, the divorce rate began to climb and family living arrangements underwent a period of rapid transition. The divorce rate rose throughout the 1960s with the upward swing accelerating during the 1970s, so that by the mid 1970s, it was higher than during peak years following World War II (Glick and Norton, 1973:303; Norton and Glick, 1979:8). Preston and others estimate that a continuation of current rates implies that as many as half the marriages contracted in the 1970s will eventually end in divorce (Preston, 1975:457; Weed, 1978; Preston and McDonald, 1979).

The high incidence of divorce during the past two decades does not mean that marriage as an institution has been abandoned. Most persons eventually do marry and four out of five divorced persons remarry (U.S. Bureau of the Census, 1975e). Throughout the 1960s the increase in remarriage rates paralleled the rise in divorce. It is the case, though, that as the divorce rate continued to rise in the 1970s, the remarriage rate turned downward (Norton and Glick, 1979). Although this may be a temporary phenomenon, it may indicate an increase in the number of years adults spend living in arrangements other than husband–wife families.

In addition to changes in marriage and divorce, substantial alterations in fertility patterns occurred in the 1960s and 1970s. Legitimate fertility rates peaked in 1957 and then dropped off dramatically. Both the decline in fertility within marriage and the increase in childbearing outside marriage contributed to the growth in the ratio of out-of-wedlock to legitimate births. By 1976, 14 percent of white and 50 percent of black births were to women who were not currently married (Bianchi and Farley, 1979:543; Ross and Sawhill, 1975:78).

The increases in divorce rates and births outside of marriage coincided with yet another change—an increase in the median age at first marriage (Ross and Sawhill, 1975:196; Norton and Glick, 1979). As young adults delayed entry into first marriages during the late 1960s and 1970s, marriages before age 25 were considerably fewer than they had been in the 1950s (Bianchi and Farley, 1979:540). As a consequence, a growing number of persons moved out of their parental households but did not immediately form their own new families.

Throughout the 1960–1976 period, the number of households grew faster than did the total population. The result was a substantial alteration in the average size and composition of households. A declining proportion included a husband–wife couple raising their dependent children—the type of household often considered the typical or average American household. In fact, by 1976 only 55 percent of all whites and 43 percent of all blacks lived in such households (see Table 3.1). On the other hand, there was a dramatic increase in the number of persons living alone and in the number residing in families headed by women. Although increases in household headship by women were parallel for whites and blacks, increases were twice as large among blacks and by 1976 black–white distributions across household type were more dissimilar than they had been in 1960.

Increases in Persons Living Alone (or with Nonrelatives)

Perhaps the most significant change in household composition in recent decades has been the increase in the number of individuals, both male and female, who either live alone or with nonrelatives, that is, the increase in the number of households headed by what the U.S. Bureau of the Census refers to as a "primary individual." Between 1960 and 1974 there were increases in the number of primary individuals of all ages, but the increase in young men who lived alone or with nonrelatives was two to three times as great as that for older men. Among women growth was largest among the elderly, although the increase among young women was also sizable (Kobrin, 1973, 1976). While the increase in the number of young adults, the delay in first marriage, the growth in the elderly population, and the sex differential in longevity explain why certain age–sex groups ac-

Table 3.1. *Distribution of Households and Persons by Race and Household Type*

	White			Black		
	1960	*1970*	*1976*	*1960*	*1970*	*1976*
			Distribution of households[a]			
Husband–wife head	75.8	70.5	66.9	61.0	51.7	44.0
With children <18	46.0	39.9	35.6	40.2	33.6	27.8
No children	29.8	30.6	31.3	20.8	18.1	16.2
Female head	16.5	20.1	22.6	27.9	34.6	40.7
Living alone	8.7	11.6	13.4	8.7	11.0	13.2
Children <18	3.5	4.3	5.3	12.9	18.0	22.1
Other	4.3	4.2	4.0	6.3	5.6	5.4
Male head	7.7	9.4	10.5	11.1	13.6	15.3
Living alone	4.7	6.0	7.1	6.4	8.3	10.1
Other	3.0	3.4	3.4	4.7	5.3	5.2
Total (sample n)	(47,112)	(55,769)	(40,378)	(4,723)	(6,145)	(4,718)

	White			Black		
	1960	1970	1976	1960	1970	1976
		Distribution of persons across household type[a]				
Husband–wife head	86.2	82.9	80.5	71.9	63.2	55.4
With children <18	65.1	60.0	55.4	59.1	51.0	43.3
No children	21.1	22.9	25.1	12.8	12.2	12.1
Female head	9.8	12.1	14.0	22.4	29.6	36.9
Living alone	2.7	3.8	4.7	2.3	3.1	4.2
With children <18	4.0	5.1	6.2	15.9	22.7	28.7
Other	3.1	3.2	3.1	4.2	3.8	4.0
Male head	4.0	5.0	5.5	5.7	7.2	7.7
Living alone	1.4	2.0	2.5	1.7	2.3	3.2
Other	2.6	3.0	3.0	4.0	4.9	4.5
Total (sample n)	(152,560)	(170,009)	(114,893)	(18,139)	(21,779)	(14,947)

[a] Expressed in percentages.

count for such a large share of the increase, demographic factors alone do not answer the question of why adults at the youngest and oldest ages have become so much more likely to form their own households than to live with relatives. Whereas in 1940 less than half of all elderly women who were not currently married lived alone, by 1970 over 70 percent of comparable women lived alone or with nonrelatives (Kobrin, 1976:136). One explanation for this increase among the elderly is that as Social Security benefits increased and low-rent housing for the elderly became more plentiful, a greater proportion could afford to maintain separate households. Work by Michael, Fuchs, and Scott (1980) supports this explanation: In their cross-state estimations, growth in income explained three-fourths of the 1950–1976 increase in the proportion of young adults living alone, and income was also the most important variable in the equation for elderly women.

Such an economic interpretation seems to assume that maintaining an independent residence is desirable, either to the person living alone, the family of that person, or both. Kobrin (1976) argues, in fact, that an important normative shift has taken place during recent decades. At a time when there are increasing numbers of extended kin who could be included in households—for example, elderly parents and adult children—there has been an increased emphasis upon independence and privacy and a decline in tolerance of nonnuclear family members.

The great increase in persons living separately from families, and the concentration of these people at the youngest and oldest stages of the life cycle, indicate two major changes: that a process of age-segregation is going on, and that there is a decreasing tolerance for family forms which include non-nuclear members. Family membership is becoming much less continuous over the life cycle, affecting the relationship between the generations (which are now much less visible to each other) and life cycle patterns of interaction generally (Kobrin, 1976:137).

Living alone is in line with social emphases on individualism, independence, and privacy. Interestingly, this trend has not been interpreted as a sign that family ties are disintegrating.

Increases in Female-Headed Families with Children

Prior to 1960, growth in the number of female primary individuals was the major source of the increase in female-headed households. Only in the last two decades has the growth in families headed by women also contributed substantially to increases in the number of households headed by women (Kobrin, 1973:798). The absolute number of female-headed families actually declined in the 1940s and increased modestly in the 1950s. The 1960s, however, were marked by substantial growth in the number of families headed by women and this upward trend accelerated in the 1970s (Ross and Sawhill, 1975).

The growth is important for several reasons. First, precarious financial circumstances characterize many female-headed families with children. In 1975, 44 percent of female-headed families with children were below official poverty thresholds, as compared with 7 percent of husband–wife families with children (U.S. Bureau of the Census, 1977e: Table 18). Second, the number and percent of all children who live with only their mothers is quite large and has been increasing. In 1976, 6.4 million white and 3.8 million black children resided with their mothers but not their fathers (U.S. Bureau of the Census, 1977b: Table 5). Living in female-headed families might be considered a somewhat temporary status but, in any case, spending a portion of childhood in a female-headed family is becoming increasingly common. Bumpass and Rindfuss (1979:54) estimate that before reaching age 16, one-sixth of all white children and three-fifths of all black children will experience their parents' marital disruption if the experience of the early 1970s continues. Finally, racial differentials in family headship by women are quite large and have widened over time. Since 1960 nonwhite female-headed families have grown twice as fast as white female-headed families, and by 1977 less than one-half of all black children lived with both parents (Johnson, 1978).

The greatest increase in female family headship has been among young women, and, increasingly, women heading families are either divorced or separated rather than widowed. In terms of the demographic components of the increase, Ross and Sawhill (1975:22–24) emphasize the increase in marital disruption and also point to the increase in out-of-wedlock births, particularly among blacks. Cutright (1974) emphasizes population growth and changes in living arrangements, that is, the increased likelihood of a woman to form a separate household following divorce or out-of-wedlock birth. Cooney (1979) suggests that although population growth and changes in living arrangements are the major factors contributing to long-term growth of white female-headed families, the rise in divorce is the key to current increases among whites. Among blacks, the increased likelihood that a couple has children when marital disruption occurs, rather than the rise in divorce per se, is a major component of the growth.

The question that arises is what, specifically, causes the accelerated growth of female-headed families, particularly among blacks. Ross and Sawhill (1975) speculate that this growth is related to

the continuing urbanization of the black population; to increased sexual activity and improved health, combined with a low level of effective contraception among teenagers; to the bleak employment prospects for black men with little education; and to the greater availability of income outside of marriage for the poorest group of black women (1975:88).

In addition, the incidence of female family headship among blacks may be overstated because of misreporting of marital status and the failure to locate and enumerate male household members.

Whether or not growth in families headed by a woman is viewed in positive or negative terms depends on whether or not the increase is seen as evidence that women, because of social and economic changes, now have greater freedom and choice in living arrangements than in the past. Cooney (1979) argues that the "voluntary" aspect of the increase may vary for women of differing race–ethnic groups.

Given the greater options and opportunities available to white females and the higher rates of remarriage, the growth of such families may be a positive indicator that women are exploring their alternatives, seeking a more congenial environment in which to grow. The rapid growth of Puerto Rican and black female headed families, on the other hand, appears to be less a "voluntary" response to opportunity for greater self-actualization and more an outcome associated with subjecting greater numbers of women to the problems and life circumstances associated with minority group status (Cooney, 1979:156).

The crucial question is what motivates both the increase in divorce, especially the increase among couples with children, and the increase in separate household formation.

Economic Factors in Female-Headed Families' Growth

The interrelationship among nonwhites of male unemployment and marital dissolution was suggested in the 1965 Moynihan report.

From 1951 to 1963, the level of Negro male unemployment was on a long-run rising trend, while at the same time following the short-run ups and downs of the business cycle. During the same period, the number of broken families in the Negro world was also on a long-run rise, with intermediate ups and downs.

. . . the series move in the same directions—ups and downs together, with a long-run rising trend—but the peaks and troughs are 1 year out of phase. Thus unemployment peaks 1 year before broken families, and so on. By plotting these series in terms of deviation from trend, and moving the unemployment curve 1 year ahead, we see the clear relation of the two otherwise seemingly unrelated series of events; the cyclical swings in unemployment have their counterpart in increases and decreases in separations (Moynihan, 1965:21).

What Moynihan failed to anticipate was the continued upward trend in separation and divorce during the late 1960s, even as the nonwhite male unemployment rate dropped to 5 percent. Marital disruption did not abate during the late 1960s when the economic status of black men improved. If one removes the long-run linear trend in marital disruption and plots year-to-year deviations from trend, fluctuations in the late 1960s and 1970s do appear somewhat responsive to fluctuations in the unemployment rate, but the correlation is not as high as that for the period studied by Moynihan (cf. Miao, 1974; Bianchi and Farley, 1979).

Most analysts would agree that the interrelation of aggregate separation rates and unemployment rates is a rather crude test of whether a husband's performance as a provider is a precipitating factor in divorce. More convincing evidence is provided by Ross and Sawhill (1975:Chapter 3). Using data on individual families from the first five years of the Panel Study of Income Dynamics, their analysis shows that if a husband experienced serious unemployment between 1965 and 1968, a couple was more likely to divorce or separate between 1968 and 1972, net of other factors, than if no such period of unemployment occurred.

It is perhaps not surprising that a husband's unemployment correlates with separation: Economic problems resulting from a husband's failure to provide earnings to a family might well exacerbate problems in other areas. Whether unemployment differentials between black and white men account for racial differences in female headship, however, remains ambiguous. It is difficult to test whether economic roles of males relate similarly to marriage and divorce probabilities among blacks and whites because black men have not yet faced employment opportunities and constraints similar to those of white men.

Much attention has been focused on the changing economic status of women as a causal factor in the increase in divorce and separation. Evidence from the Seattle–Denver income maintenance experiments suggests that, as women's income outside of marriage increases, at least if increases are modest, more marital disruption occurs (Hannan, Tuma, and Groeneveld, 1977, 1978). Within the experiment, families are assigned to either a control situation or one of three guaranteed support levels. Couples are guaranteed a certain level of support whether they remain together or not. The findings are that

for whites the low support treatment almost doubles the rate of dissolution; this effect is significant at the .05 level. The next higher support level raises the dissolution rate by 56%; this increase is not statistically significant. The high support actually decreases the rate but is not significant at even the .10 level. A similar pattern holds for blacks. Both low and medium support levels more than double the rate. Both effects are significant at the .05 level. The high support has a considerably smaller and insignificant effect (Hannan, Tuma, and Groeneveld, 1978:613).

The low-support experimental condition in the income maintenance experiments provide a level of support that is little different from the combination of Aid to Families with Dependent Children (AFDC) and food stamps. The finding of a strong relation between the low level of guaranteed income and marital dissolution is in contrast to much of the work on the relation of AFDC and female headship. Moore and Caldwell (1976) found no effect of either the availability or the level of AFDC benefits on the out-of-wedlock childbearing of adolescents. Evidence on the relation of AFDC to marital disruption is somewhat mixed but investigations by Cherlin (1978) as well as Sawhill, et al.

(1975) found no effect of AFDC benefit levels on the likelihood of a marital disruption. Hoffman and Holmes (1976), using the same data as Sawhill and her colleagues but with a different model specification, did find marital disruption to be higher in states with high AFDC benefit levels, but differences between high- and low-benefit states were not great. The most convincing evidence is that higher levels of AFDC support are associated with a delay in remarriage (MacDonald and Sawhill, 1978; G. Duncan, 1976). But even this correlation may be spurious: Amount of support is connected with the number of children a woman has and the greater the number of children, the less time and energy a woman has to devote to a marital search. Potential marriage partners may also be unwilling to assume responsibility for those children. In sum, if a relationship between AFDC and female headship exists, the availability of AFDC is probably facilitative of separate household formation rather than the cause motivating a divorce or out-of-wedlock birth. In this sense, AFDC is similar in effect to increasing women's earnings (Ross and Sawhill, 1975:117). Both provide women with an alternative source of support outside marriage, that is, with more independence.

It is this "independence effect" that Hannan and his associates (1978) point to as the key to understanding why low, AFDC-like levels of support in the income maintenance experiments result in the highest levels of marital dissolution. At low levels of support, the independence effect is stronger than the competing "income effect." The income effect refers to the well-established inverse relation between a family's socioeconomic status and the likelihood of divorce. Whether because of the absence of marital tension due to economic strain, the greater costs involved in marital dissolution among the more affluent, or some cultural factor such as a differential social class valuation of marriage, higher-income couples are much less likely to separate than lower-income couples.

Competing with this income effect is the independence effect. If a woman has income available to her apart from her husband's earnings—whether in the form of her own earnings or welfare benefits—she is in a better economic position to end an unsatisfying marriage. The explanation implicitly offered by the income maintenance experiments is that, at the low level of guaranteed support, the independence effect outweighs the income effect. Why a low level of guaranteed income should facilitate disruption when a similar level of AFDC support does not is curious. The researchers offer four possible explanations: Income maintenance involves less stigma, is clearly outlined for participants, entails lower transaction costs than AFDC, and perhaps most significant,

the informational content of income maintenance programs may have another effect, that of introducing a shock to the pre-experimental equilibrium. The literature on marriage indicates that many unhappy and unfulfilling marriages are stable for long periods of time because the partners reach some kind of accommodation (Hannan, Tuma, and Groeneveld, 1977:1208–1209).

In short, there exists a body of research that suggests that both men's unemployment and women's access to income from sources other than a man's earnings facilitate marital disruption, but the key word seems to be "facilitate" rather than "cause." Economic strain, which can be intensified by a husband's unemployment, can affect the emotional, psychological, and relational functioning of a family unit. And a modicum of financial independence gives a woman the option of removing herself— and her children—from an unsatisfying family situation.

Effects of Changing Living Arrangements

As a result of the growth in the number of households and shifts in the household living arrangements of individuals, the

Table 3.2. Household Size by Race and Household Type

Average size	1960	1970	1976	Δ 1960– 1976
All				
White	3.24	3.05	2.85	−.39
Black	3.84	3.54	3.17	−.67
Mean gap	.60	.49	.32	
Husband–wife head				
White	3.68	3.58	3.42	−.26
Black	4.53	4.33	3.99	−.54
Mean gap	.85	.75	.57	
Female head				
White	1.92	1.83	1.77	−.15
Black	3.08	3.03	2.87	−.21
Mean gap	1.16	1.20	1.17	
Male head				
White	1.68	1.64	1.48	−.20
Black	1.97	1.88	1.59	−.38
Mean gap	.29	.22	.11	

average size of households declined between 1960 and 1976. Throughout the 1960–1976 period there was a substantial racial difference in household size, due to differential fertility, to the depressed economic situation of and discrimination faced by blacks (which resulted in more "doubling up" of black families within households), and perhaps to differential preferences in living arrangements. As can be seen in Table 3.2, although household size was at each point larger for blacks, between 1960 and 1976 household size declined more rapidly for blacks than for whites.

As I have said, the decline in fertility within marriage, the increase in divorce and in births out-of-wedlock altered the composition of households. For both races, the proportion of husband–wife households with children, either the head's own or others, declined while the proportion of female-headed households with children increased (see Table 3.3). By 1976, 23 percent of white compared to 54 percent of black female-headed households had dependents residing in them. Among blacks and whites, the increase came about because of the increasing probability of having one's own child or children present. The proportion of households with other children present actually declined, although black female-headed households were still much more likely to have other children present in 1976 than were comparable white households.

Hill (1977) has documented the higher incidence among blacks of related children living in households in which the head is not the parent of all the children—a racial difference noted in Table 3.3. He refers to this as a practice of "informal adoption" within the black community whereby relatives provide for children when the child's own parents are unable to do so and argues that this is a phenomenon particularly characteristic of black family structure.

Black households in the three years studied were more likely to have dependent children present than were white households, and changes over time served to widen this differential. That is, in 1960, about 5 percent more black than white households had children in them whereas in 1976, the racial difference was 10 percentage points (see Table 3.3). When analysis is restricted to households with children, as it is in Table 3.4, it becomes evident that the racial difference in the average number of children declined both in husband–wife and female-headed households with dependent children. By 1976 the ratio of dependent children to adults in black husband–wife households with children was actually quite similar to that for comparable white households—close to one child per adult on aver-

Table 3.3. Racial Differences in the Proportion of Households with Children under 18 Present, Head's Own Children under 18 Present, and Other Children under 18 Present[a]

	Proportion of households with children <18			Proportion of households with head's own children <18			Proportion of households with children <18 other than head's own children		
	1960	1970	1976	1960	1970	1976	1960	1970	1976
All									
White	50	45	42	48	44	40	3	3	2
Black	55	54	52	46	48	45	14	11	11
Gap	−5	−9	−10	−2	−4	−5	−11	−8	−9
Husband–wife head									
White	61	57	53	59	55	52	3	3	2
Black	66	65	63	58	59	58	14	11	10
Gap	−5	−8	−10	−1	−4	−6	−11	−8	−8
Female head									
White	21	21	23	18	19	21	7	3	3
Black	46	52	54	34	44	46	18	14	14
Gap	−25	−31	−31	−16	−25	−25	−11	−11	−11

[a] Expressed in percentages.

Table 3.4. *Household Size, Number of Children, and Ratios of Children to Adults for All Black and White Households, Husband–Wife Households with Children, and Female-Headed Households with Children*

	Average household size			Average number of children			Ratio of children to adults		
	1960	1970	1976	1960	1970	1976	1960	1970	1976
All									
White	3.24	3.05	2.85	1.15	1.04	.87	.55	.52	.44
Black	3.84	3.54	3.17	1.68	1.54	1.29	.78	.77	.69
Mean gap	.60	.49	.32	.53	.50	.42			
Husband–wife head with children <18									
White	4.58	4.59	4.43	2.32	2.31	2.12	1.03	1.01	.92
Black	5.65	5.37	4.94	3.14	2.90	2.48	1.25	1.17	1.01
Mean gap	1.07	.78	.51	.82	.59	.36			
Female head with children <18									
White	3.67	3.63	3.36	2.04	2.16	1.96	1.25	1.47	1.40
Black	4.73	4.46	4.12	2.89	2.81	2.58	1.57	1.77	1.68
Mean gap	1.06	.83	.76	.85	.65	.62			

age. Dependency ratios in female-headed households were 1.40 for whites and 1.68 for blacks, considerably higher than the one child per adult ratio in husband–wife families.

Whereas child/adult dependency ratios declined throughout the period for husband–wife households, they increased between 1960 and 1970 for female-headed households. Dependency ratios declined somewhat for black and white female-headed households in the 1970s, but the 1976 ratios remained higher than they had been in 1960. Increasingly, women, both black and white, were raising children without the aid of any other adult in the household.

Summary

The 1960–1976 period was one of considerable change in the living arrangements of individuals. For women, the most important change was the increase in the proportion who headed households as family heads or women living alone or with nonrelatives. Headship rates remain higher for black women and the increase between 1960 and 1976 was also greater among black women. During the 1970s there was an associated decline in the proportion of white women who lived with their husbands, but it was much smaller than the comparable change among blacks. By 1977 only 44 percent of black women 18 to 64 years of age were married and living with their husbands, compared to 71 percent of white women (Bianchi and Farley, 1979).

For men, the major change between 1960 and 1976 was the increase in the number, black and white, who lived alone or with nonrelatives. This was the corollary of the increase in household headship among women.

About 90 percent of all white children in 1960 lived with both parents, but by 1976 this figure had fallen slightly to 86 percent. A much greater shift occurred among blacks: In 1960, 66 percent of black children lived in families with both parents but this declined to just under 50 percent in 1976. The major offsetting change has been the increasing propensity of children to live in families that include their mother but not their father. In 1976, 40 percent of the black children under 18 years of age and 12 percent of the white were in such living arrangements.[1]

Why are 1960–1976 shifts in household living arrangements of men, women, and their children of importance to the study of racial inequality and change over time in economic well-being? As I discussed in Chapter 2, assessment of household economic well-being implies measurement of household income in relation to member needs. Changes that occurred between 1960 and 1976 altered each of these components. On the one hand, there was a large increase in the number of one-person households as an increasing number of young and elderly adults lived alone. The upswing in divorce resulted in the frequent splitting of one larger unit into two smaller households. The decline in fertility within marriage reduced the average number of dependents in husband–wife households. Hence, between 1960 and 1976, average household need levels of whites and blacks were reduced considerably. On the other hand, the types of households that increased dramatically were those most likely to have low household incomes. That is, much of the growth in one person units was not among persons at their peak earning power but rather among elderly women and young adults. The other major increase, the growth in households comprised of a woman and her dependent children represented an increase in households with high ratios of dependent children to potential wage earners. Growing numbers of children, particularly black children, lived apart from a male wage earner.

Chapter 4

Changing Sources of Household Income of Blacks and Whites

Between 1960 and 1976 not only were there shifts in household size and composition; but there were also important changes in the sources of household income. By 1976 almost a fifth of household income, on average, came from sources other than the earnings of household members, whereas only 11 percent had come from other sources in 1960. In husband–wife households, labor force participation on the part of wives increased dramatically during this period, and the portion of household income provided by the wife's earnings rose for both races. In male- and female-headed households, due in part to the increase in men and women living alone, there was considerable decline in earnings from anyone other than the head. As husband–wife households became ever more likely to have at least two earners, other type households, in particular female-headed households with dependent children, became increasingly likely to have either one or no earner at all in residence. As dissimilarities in the labor force activity grew between husband–wife and female-headed households, black–white distributions across household type widened.

Sources of Household Income, 1960–1976

Table 4.1 reports the average income levels and the proportion of income from earnings and other sources for all black

Table 4.1. Sources of Income in Black and White Households[a]

	1960		1976	
	White	*Black*	*White*	*Black*
All				
Income (mean)	$11,218	$6,525	$14,335	$9,222
From earnings	88.7	89.0	82.6	80.9
From other sources	11.3	11.0	17.4	19.1
Husband–wife head				
Income (mean)	$12,562	$7,667	$17,110	$12,796
From earnings	90.8	92.3	86.2	88.1
(Husbands)	(72.6)	(65.3)	(66.6)	(57.3)
(Wives)	(11.2)	(16.0)	(14.3)	(23.5)
(Other adults)	(6.6)	(10.4)	(4.9)	(6.9)
(Teenagers)	(0.4)	(0.6)	(0.4)	(0.4)
From other sources	9.2	7.7	13.8	11.9
Female head				
Income (mean)	$6,266	$4,382	$7,414	$5,835
From earnings	72.1	77.7	59.6	64.2
(Female head)	(44.6)	(39.5)	(44.0)	(46.6)
(Other adults)	(27.0)	(37.1)	(15.2)	(17.0)
(Teenagers)	(0.4)	(1.1)	(0.4)	(0.6)
From other sources	27.9	22.3	40.4	35.8
Male head				
Income (mean)	$8,582	$5,636	$11,499	$7,930
From earnings	83.0	86.9	80.1	80.4
(Male head)	(64.8)	(64.9)	(67.5)	(66.5)
(Others)	(18.2)	(22.0)	(12.6)	(13.9)
From other sources	17.9	13.1	19.9	19.6

[a] All dollar figures have been converted to 1975 dollars using the Consumer Price Index. All other figures are percentages of total dollar amounts.

Table 4.2. *Sources of Income Other Than Current Earnings in Black and White Households in 1976*

	Average amount in all households[a]	Proportion of all households with this source[b]	Average receipts in households receiving this type income[a]
Veterans' payments/ unemployment[c]			
Whites	$300	18.7%	$1,606
Blacks	280	17.7	1,579
Public assistance[d]			
Whites	109	6.4	1,702
Blacks	563	27.0	2,090
Social Security[e]			
Whites	846	27.9	3,031
Blacks	612	25.7	2,383
Retirement[f]			
Whites	424	11.1	3,832
Blacks	153	4.8	3,190
Other[g]			
Whites	821	56.2	1,462
Blacks	149	18.8	800

[a] Expressed in 1975 dollars.

[b] Expressed in percentages.

[c] Includes veterans' payments of all kinds, unemployment insurance benefits, and workmens' compensation.

[d] Includes amount received from federal, state, and local public programs such as aid for dependent children, old age assistance, general assistance, and aid to the blind or totally disabled; excludes medical care.

[e] Includes U.S. government payments to retired persons, to dependents of deceased insured workers, or to disabled workers; excludes Medicare reimbursements.

[f] Includes retirement pensions from private employers, unions, and governmental agencies.

and white households, husband–wife households, female- and male-headed households in 1960 and 1976. All wage, salary, and farm and business income received by persons 14 years and older in the household during the year preceding the census survey are included in earnings. Cash transfers to household members from public assistance, Social Security, railroad retirement, private pensions, veteran's payments, unemployment and workmen's compensation, income from alimony, rents, dividends, and other contributions from outside the household during the preceding calendar year are referred to as sources other than earnings.

Sources Other Than Earnings / Both black and white households obtained similar portions of their income from earnings and from other sources. The share of income from sources other than earnings increased between 1960 and 1976 so that by 1976 these other sources amounted to 20 percent of household income, on average. There were considerable differences by household type in the proportion of income from nonearnings sources; husband–wife households obtained about 12–14 percent, male-headed households about 20 percent, and female-headed households about 35–40 percent in 1976.

A detailed inspection of racial differences in receipt of other types of income is possible only for 1976. As can be seen in Table 4.2, the one type of income received more often in black than in white households was public assistance income. Whereas 27 percent of black households received public assistance income, only 6.4 percent of white households did, and average receipts were correspondingly lower in white than in black

---

[8] Includes interest, dividends, and other regular payments such as net rental income, private welfare payments, alimony or child support, and regular contributions from persons not members of the household. Excludes receipts from sale of personal property, capital gains, lump sum insurance, or inheritance payments or payments in-kind.

Table 4.3. Racial Differences in Receipts from Earnings Income Sources

| | Proportion of households with earnings[a] | | | Average amount of earnings in households with earnings[b] | | | |
	1960	1976	Δ1960–1976	1960	1976	Δ1960–1976 $	Δ1960–1976 %
All							
White	87.1%	80.9%	− 6.1%	$11,420	$14,653	+$3,232	+28.3%
Black	87.0	76.3	−10.8	6,679	9,783	+ 3,104	+46.5
Racial Difference (W−B)	0.1	4.6		4,742	4,870		
Ratio (B/W)				.585	.668		
Husband–wife head							
White	93.1	89.3	− 3.8	12,257	16,541	+ 4,284	+35.0
Black	94.1	90.2	− 3.9	7,522	12,495	+ 4,973	+60.2
Racial Difference (W−B)	1.0	.9		4,735	4,046		
Ratio (B/W)				.614	.755		
Female head							
White	64.4	57.6	− 6.8	7,013	7,674	+ 661	+ 9.4
Black	73.3	62.5	−10.8	4,650	6,001	+ 1,351	+29.1
Racial Difference (W−B)	8.9	4.9		2,363	1,673		
Ratio (B/W)				.663	.782		
Male head							
White	76.3	77.3	+ 1.0	9,333	11,949	+ 2,616	+28.0
Black	82.7	73.0	− 9.7	5,923	8,731	+ 2,808	+47.4
Racial Difference	1.0	9.7		3,410	3,218		
Ratio (B/W)				.635	.731		

[a]Expressed in percentages.
[b]Expressed in 1975 dollars.

households. This racial differential has also been documented with data from the Panel Study of Income Dynamics (Katherine Dickinson, 1974).

On the other hand, white households were substantially more likely than black households to receive income from sources such as rent, interest, annuities, alimony, and other regular contributions from persons not members of the household. Average receipts from these sources in white households were around $600 higher than in black, and whereas over half of white households received at least one of these other types of income, less than a fifth of black households received any income from these sources.

Similarly, white households receiving either Social Security or other retirement income averaged about $600 more from these sources than did black households. Because Social Security and retirement income represent the financial benefits of prior attachment to the labor force, this $600 difference gives some indication of the long term cost to blacks of both their higher rates of unemployment, more frequent employment in marginal jobs, and their depressed wage rates relative to whites. Thompson (1979:20), in an analysis of racial differences in coverage and benefits from private pensions, has shown that blacks are much less likely than whites to have been in occupations and industries with private pension plans. Blacks are also less likely than whites to have the requisite number of years and recency of employment to qualify for benefits when plans are available. The extent to which these racial differentials are a result of discrimination remains an open question.

Income from Earnings / Although income from sources other than earnings grew in importance between 1960 and 1976, 80 percent of black and white household income, on average, still came from the earnings of household members in 1976. Table 4.3 presents both the proportion of all households that received income from earnings and the average amount received (in 1975 dollars) in 1960 and 1976. Data are shown separately for husband–wife, female-, and male-headed households.

The vast majority of both white and black households (i.e., 87 percent) received income from earnings in 1960. By 1976 the proportion of white households with earnings dropped to 80 percent; that of blacks dropped even farther to 76 percent. Declines occurred in each type of household. The decline in the proportion of husband–wife households with earnings was similar for both races and resulted primarily from the increase in the proportion of households comprised of an elderly, non-wage-earning couple. In female-headed households the decline was larger among blacks, and in male-headed households, whereas there was no decline in the proportion with earnings among whites, there was a 10 percentage point decrease among blacks.

Although the *overall* racial gap in average amounts from earnings increased slightly between 1960 and 1976, within each type of household the average racial gap narrowed and the ratio of black to white household earnings increased. As has been noted elsewhere (cf. Farley, 1977; Green and Welniak, 1980), because the shift out of husband–wife households (i.e., households with relatively high probabilities of receiving earnings and with high average receipts) was more accentuated among blacks, overall income and earnings improvements of blacks vis-à-vis whites were dampened, particularly in the 1970s.

Labor Force Participation and Earnings of Household Members

Tables 4.4 through 4.8 provide a more detailed look at labor force attachment and earnings within husband–wife, male-, and female-headed households and show the average annual hours worked and average earnings for the preceding year in households with particular types of earners. The estimate of annual hours worked is actually a proxy since the 1960 census did not ascertain the previous year's hours of employment. Rather, data were collected on the number of hours a person worked in the week prior to the census and the number of weeks a person worked in the past year. Estimates of annual hours worked were arrived at by multiplying those two factors.

When persons reported working some weeks during the previous year *and* had earnings for that period, but were not at work in the week prior to the census, a weekly number of hours was imputed to them. Multiple classification analysis was used to arrive at an estimate of mean weekly hours of work for employed persons of a given age, race, sex, years of schooling completed, occupation, and marital status. Even though the imputation introduces some further error into the calculation of hours worked, it seemed preferable to excluding those not at work in the week prior to the census. Exclusion would typically underestimate the number of earners who contribute to household income and overestimate the average number of hours contributed by workers. Eliminating persons who were not working in the week prior to the census would have been particularly serious for assessing the work contributions of women and children. Their earnings contributions are of importance to households, but their labor force participation is less often year round than is the case for males. Therefore, they frequently are not found to be at work in the week preceding the census, though they contributed to earnings in the previous year.[1]

Husband–Wife Households / In 1960 husbands of both races were equally likely to have worked in the preceding year. Approximately 89 percent had some earnings in 1959 (see Table 4.4). Proportions declined for both races between 1960 and 1976, and in 1976 black husbands were slightly less likely to

Table 4.4. Racial Differences in Earnings and Labor Force Participation of Household Members in Husband–Wife Households[a]

	Proportion of households with others[a]			Proportion with household head/other which received earnings from head/other[b]		
	1960	1976	Δ1960–1976	1960	1976	Δ1960–1976
Husbands						
White				89.5%	84.5%	− 5.0%
Black				89.4	82.0	− 7.4
Racial difference (W–B)				0.1	2.5	
Ratio (B/W)						
Wives						
White				35.5	49.4	+14.1
Black				50.3	59.9	+ 9.6
Racial difference (W–B)				−15.0	−10.5	
Ratio (B/W)						
Other Adults						
White	20.9	22.0	+1.1	71.5	78.5	+ 7.0
Black	30.1	27.3	−2.8	66.0	69.9	+ 3.9
Racial difference (W–B)	− 9.2	− 5.3		5.5	8.6	
Ratio (B/W)						
Teenagers, 14–17						
White	18.9	20.8	+1.9	31.0	43.9	+12.9
Black	21.0	24.7	+3.7	24.1	26.3	+ 2.2
Racial difference (W–B)	− 2.1	− 3.9		6.9	17.6	
Ratio (B/W)						

[a]Estimates of hours and earnings of other adults and teenagers represent the mean of the sum of hours and earnings from adults and teenagers other than the husband and wife coheads.

Average annual hours worked by head/other who worked previous year			Average earnings from head/other who had earnings previous year[c]			
1960	*1976*	*Δ1960–1976*	*1960*	*1976*	*Δ1960–1976*	
2,098	2,062	− 36	$10,201	$13,487	+$3,286	32.2%
1,838	1,832	− 6	5,601	8,936	+ 3,335	59.5
260	230		4,600	4,551		
.88	.89		.55	.66		
1,298	1,297	− 1	3,972	4,967	+ 995	25.1
1,139	1,393	+254	2,427	5,019	+ 2,592	106.8
159	− 96		1,545	− 52		
.88	1.070		.61	1.00		
1,807	1,405	−402	5,539	4,837	− 702	− 12.7
1,814	1,445	−369	4,032	4,793	− 761	− 18.9
− 7	− 40		1,507	44		
1.00	1.03		.73	.99		
387	295	− 92	991	809	− 182	− 18.4
536	211	−325	852	821	− 31	− 3.6
− 149	84		139	− 12		
1.39	.72		.86	1.01		

[b] Expressed in percentages.
[c] Expressed in 1975 dollars.

have had earnings during the previous year than were whites. Black husbands, when they did work, worked about 88 percent of the hours reported in 1960 for white husbands but earned only 55 percent as much. In 1976 black husbands who worked still averaged about 89 percent as many hours of labor activity as white husbands but earned about 66 percent as much.

Both because of the low earnings levels of black husbands and because of the relatively large proportion of black wives who contributed to household earnings, in 1960 black wives' proportional contribution to household income was higher than for white wives: 16 percent, on average, as compared to 11 percent (see Table 4.1). By 1976 the proportional contribution of both black and white wives had risen: from 11 to 14 percent for whites and from 16 to 24 percent for blacks. The proportion of wives who earned income increased for both races between 1960 and 1976, but the increase was actually greater for white wives. Earnings levels of white and black wives were not significantly different by 1976 and averaged around $5,000.

Earnings from other adult members of households accounted for about 7 percent of income in white households and 10 percent in black in 1960. This declined some—to 5 and 7 percent, respectively—in 1976. When other adults were in residence, white households were more likely to receive earnings from them than were black households and the racial differential was greater in 1976. Contributions of earners 14–17 were not a very significant factor in the annual income in most husband–wife households, though in the small portion of households with such earnings, $800–$1,000, on average, came from teenagers.

Male-Headed Households / A small proportion of households—8 percent for whites and 11 percent for blacks in 1960— were male-headed households but the proportion grew between 1960 and 1976 (to 11 percent for whites and 15 percent for blacks). This change occurred because of the increase in the number of males living alone.

Whereas in 1960 black male heads of households were more likely than whites to have earnings, by 1976 this relationship had reversed (see Table 4.5). As with black husbands, when black male heads did work, they worked fewer hours than did whites—about 88–89 percent as many hours. At each time point, male household heads of both races averaged around 90 percent the annual hours of husbands.

The earnings of black male heads were substantially less than for whites. That is, although they worked about 90 percent as much as white male household heads, their average earnings were only 61 percent those of whites in 1960 and 73 percent those of whites in 1976. Over the period, whites obtained a 33 percent increase in real earnings and blacks a 58 percent increase.

The proportion of male-headed households with other adults in residence was not very different for blacks and whites, slightly higher for blacks at each point. A significant change was the 7 percentage point drop between 1960–1976 in the proportion of both black and white households with other adults, that is, the rise in the proportion of single-person households. Interestingly, in 1960, when other adults were present in black households, they were substantially more likely to provide some earnings than were other adults in white households. This situation reversed rather dramatically between 1960 and 1976. The white proportion increased from 62 to 77 percent whereas for blacks it declined from 76 to 63 percent.

Female-Headed Households / Between 1960 and 1976 the proportion of all white households that were female headed rose from 17 to 23 percent. The increase in black households with a female head was even more substantial—from 28 percent in 1960 to 41 percent of all households in 1976. Black female

Table 4.5. Racial Differences in Earnings and Labor Force Participation of Household Members in Male-Headed Households [a]

	Proportion of households with others [c]			Proportion with household head/others which received earnings from head/others [c]		
Total [b]	1960	1976	Δ1960–1976	1960	1976	Δ1960–1976
Male head						
White				70.4%	74.0%	+ 3.6%
Black				75.6	69.1	− 6.5
Racial difference (W–B)				− 5.2	4.9	
Ratio (B/W)						
Other adults						
White	35.6%	28.8%	−6.8%	61.8	77.0	+15.2
Black	37.9	30.8	−7.1	76.4	62.8	−13.6
Racial difference (W–B)	− 2.3	− 2.0		−14.6	14.2	
Ratio (B/W)						
Men living alone						
White				68.8	70.3	+ 1.5
Black				77.5	65.1	−12.4
Racial difference (W–B)				− 8.7	5.2	
Ratio (B/W)						

[a] Estimates of hours and earnings of other adults represent the sum of hours worked and earnings from adults other than the male head.

[b] The number of teenagers living in male headed households is so small that earnings estimates were considered too unreliable to report.

heads were more likely than white female heads to have earnings at both points (see Table 4.6), but this racial difference for all female heads is somewhat misleading because the proportion of white female heads who were elderly was much greater than for blacks. For example, in 1976, 40 percent of white female

	Average annual hours worked by head/others who worked previous year			Average earnings from head/others who had earnings previous year[d]		
		Δ1960–			Δ1960–1976	
1960	1976	1976	1960	1976	$	%
1,814	1,867	+ 53	$7,895	$10,494	+$2,599	32.9%
1,605	1,633	+ 28	4,833	7,625	+ 2,787	57.6
209	234		3,057	2,869		
.89	.88		.61	.73		
2,169	1,737	−432	7,013	6,481	− 532	− 7.6
1,775	1,562	−213	4,169	5,655	+ 1,486	+35.6
394	175		2,844	826		
.82	.90		.59	.87		
1,760	1,830		7,609	10,088	+ 2,479	32.5
1,605	1,576		4,569	7,528	+ 2,959	64.8
155	254		3,040	2,560		
.91	.86		.60	.75		

[c]Expressed in percentages.
[d]Expressed in 1975 dollars.

heads were 65 or older whereas only 20 percent of black female heads were elderly.

While the proportion of all white female heads who were wage earners changed little between 1960 and 1976, the proportion of all black female heads with earnings declined by 7 per-

Table 4.6. Racial Differences in Earnings and Labor Force Participation of Household Members in Female-Headed Households[a]

	Proportion of households with others[b]			Proportion with household head/others which received earnings from head/others[b]		
	1960	1976	Δ1960–1976	1960	1976	Δ1960–1976
Female head						
White				51.6%	50.9%	− 0.7%
Black				60.7	53.4	− 7.3
Racial difference (W−B)				− 8.1	− 2.5	
Ratio (B/W)						
Other adults						
White	34.7%	24.2%	−10.5%	70.9	70.9	0.0
Black	45.9	32.3	−13.6	74.8	59.8	−15.0
Racial difference (W−B)	−11.2	− 8.1		− 3.9	11.1	
Ratio (B/W)						
Teenagers						
White	9.2	9.3	+ 0.1	30.8	41.7	+10.9
Black	17.8	22.4	+ 4.6	26.9	25.8	− 1.1
Racial difference (W−B)	− 8.6	−13.0		3.9	15.9	
Ratio (B/W)						

[a] Estimates of hours and earnings of other adults and teenagers represent the sum of hours worked and earnings from adults and teenagers.

centage points. The average number of hours worked by female heads did not change much between 1960 and 1976 for either race. In 1960, even though black female heads worked almost as many hours as whites, they earned only 55 percent as much. Average earnings of white female heads increased by 20 percent between 1960 and 1976 whereas earnings for black females increased by 73 percent. Thus by 1976 average earnings of black female heads were 80 percent those of whites. Earnings in-

Average annual hours worked by head/other who worked previous year			Average earnings from head/other who had earnings previous year[c]		Δ1960–1970	
1960	1976	Δ1960–1976	1960	1976	$	%
1,606	1,586	− 20	$5,340	$6,406	+$1,066	20.0%
1,397	1,423	+ 26	2,947	5,099	+ 2,152	23.0
209	163		2,393	1,307		
.87	.90		.55	.80		
2,119	1,658	−461	6,844	6,570	− 274	− 4.0
1,994	1,564	−430	4,636	5,125	+ 489	+12.2
125	94		2,208	1,445		
.94	.94		.68	.78		
365	280	− 75	967	809	− 158	−16.3
634	179	−455	1,028	640	− 388	−37.7
− 279	101		− 61	169		
1.79	.64		1.06	.79		

[b] Expressed in percentages.
[c] Expressed in 1975 dollars.

creases for black wives were also substantial and this gain coincides with the findings reported elsewhere (cf. Farley, 1977) that among women there has been substantial narrowing—perhaps even some reversal—of the racial earnings gap.

As with male-headed households, more black than white female-headed households had other adults present at each point, but over time there was a significant decline in the supply of other adult earners in both black and white female-headed

Table 4.7. Presence of Earners Additional to the Head in Black and White Female-Headed Households with Dependent Children

	1960	1976	Δ1960–1976[a]	
Proportion with other adults[a]				
White	40.3%	28.8%		−11.5%
Black	50.2	31.9		−18.3
Racial difference (W−B)	− 9.9	− 3.1		
Proportion of households with other adults which received earnings from others[a]				
White	75.9	78.2		+ 2.3
Black	77.4	61.7		−15.7
Racial difference (W−B)	− 1.5	16.5		
Average annual hours worked by others in households with other workers				
White	2,154	1,478	− 676	−34.1
Black	1,989	1,510	− 479	−24.1
Racial difference (W−B)	165	− 32		
Ratio (B/W)	.92	1.02		
Average earnings from others in households with earnings from others[b]				
White	$6,235	$5,537	−$698	−11.9
Black	4,236	4,678	+ 442	+10.4
Racial difference (W−B)	1,999	859		
Ratio (B/W)	.68	.84		

[a] Expressed in percentages.
[b] Expressed in 1975 dollars.

households. In 1976 only a quarter of white female-headed households contained adults additional to the head, down from over a third in 1960. For black female-headed households, not only was there a decline in the proportion of households with other adults (from nearly 46 percent in 1960 to about 32 percent in 1976); but there was also a decline in the proportion that received earnings from those other adults. Part of this decline reflects the growth in one-person households, but, as can be seen in Table 4.7, women raising dependent children were increasingly likely to be providing for those dependents without the aid of additional household earners. In 1960 around 30 percent of white and 40 percent of black female-headed households with children had earnings from others in the household.[2] By 1976, the proportions had declined to around 20 percent.

In Table 4.8, changes in the labor force activity of subgroups of female heads are presented. Overall, black female heads were more likely to work in 1960 and in 1976 than were white female heads but this was not the case in all types of female-headed households. For female heads living alone it was the case that, both in 1960 and 1976, blacks were more likely to be working than whites, although when they worked they averaged fewer hours and earned less. For other female heads, however, particularly those with dependent children, white females, who had been less likely to work in 1960, were more likely than black women to be at work in 1976.

Summary

Between 1960 and 1976 sources of income other than the current earnings of household members became more important for white and black households. Both in 1960 and in 1976 female-headed households relied on nonearned sources to a greater extent than did either husband–wife- or male-headed households, and the increase in reliance was much greater among female-headed households than among other households. This gain no doubt resulted both from the growth in the number of elderly women living alone and the increase in women raising children without a spouse present.

Table 4.8. Earnings and Labor Force Participation of Subgroups of Female Heads

	Proportion who had earnings[a]			Average annual hours of female heads who worked			Average earnings of female heads with earnings[b]			
			Δ1960–1976			Δ1960–1976			Δ1960–1976	
	1960	1976		1960	1976		1960	1976	$	%
Women who live alone										
White	49.6%	43.6%	– 6.0%	1,627	1,575	– 52	$5,575	$6,567	+$ 992	17.8%
Black	58.4	48.4	–10.0	1,419	1,438	+ 19	3,182	5,328	+ 2,146	67.4
Racial difference (W–B)	– 8.8	– 4.8		208	137		2,393	1,239		
Ratio (B/W)				.87	.91		.57	.81		
Female heads with children <18										
White	60.0	66.0	+ 6.0	1,523	1,553	+ 30	4,551	5,890	+ 1,339	29.4
Black	63.1	56.1	– 7.0	1,375	1,364	– 11	2,520	4,807	+ 2,287	90.8
Racial difference (W–B)	– 3.1	9.9		148	189		2,031	1,083		
Ratio (B/W)				.90	.88		.55	.82		
All other female heads										
White	48.8	55.8	+ 7.0	1,644	1,669	+ 25	6,012	6,793	+ 781	13.0
Black	59.7	54.3	– 5.4	1,416	1,635	+219	3,353	5,822	+ 2,469	73.6
Racial difference (W–B)	–10.9	1.5		228	34		2,659	971		
Ratio (B/W)				.86	.98		.56	.86		

[a] Expressed in percentages.
[b] Expressed in 1975 dollars.

As far as the earned component of household income, in husband–wife households, earnings from the wife increased in importance. In other types of households, earnings of the household head became more significant as fewer households had other adult earners present. Both the increase in wives' labor force participation and the growth in the number of households in which the only available earner was a woman meant that a growing number of households, particularly black households, relied in part or in total on a female wage earner.

Chapter 5

Changing Employment and Earnings of Householders

Earnings of husbands, wives, male, and female heads are crucial components of economic well-being in a majority of households. Hence, any analysis of racial inequality in household well-being must consider racial differentials in the determinants of labor force participation and earnings of household heads, as well as changes over time in these determinants. For my purposes in this chapter, analysis of males comprises husbands, men who live alone, and men who head households without a spouse present. Included among females are wives, women who live alone, and other female heads. In order to remind the reader of the composite nature of the groups of males and females analyzed and to avoid confusion with terminology used in earlier chapters, males and females are referred to as householders. Specifically, for householders under 65 years of age, the focus is on three areas.

1. *Participation in the labor force.* What is the racial differential in the proportion of nonelderly householders who work outside the home and has this changed over time? Do household/family structure variables bear any relation to labor force participation and is the relationship the same for both races?

2. *Hours of work.* For those in the labor force, do household/family status variables appear to influence the number of hours a householder works?

3. *Earnings.* How have earnings changed for nonelderly

black and white, male and female householders? How much of the race and sex differential in earnings can be explained by factors known to influence earnings such as differences in educational attainment, occupation, and work experience?

Labor Force Participation of Householders

Age profiles of male and female householders who worked in 1959, 1969, and 1975 and worked an estimated 2,000 or more hours in those years (worked full time) show a substantial decline in labor force participation for all race–sex groupings after age 60. Figures 5.1 and 5.2 present proportions of householders working and working full time by age, race, sex, and year. As expected, males work a larger proportion of their adult lives than females. Whereas for males, labor force participation declined for most age groups between 1960 and 1976, for females, labor force participation rates increased since 1960.[1] The increase has been particularly large among white women of child-bearing age.

Table 5.1 presents the overall proportion of householders under 65 who both worked during the years prior to the surveys and who worked full time. Although the proportion of men who worked the previous year dropped from 1960 to 1976 and was slightly lower for blacks than for whites, most male household heads (94 percent of white and 86 percent of black) reported some hours in 1976.

For women the racial differential was the opposite of that for men. That is, black women were both more often employed and more often employed full time, although the racial differentials for percent employed were considerably narrower in 1976 than in 1960. In 1960, about 44 percent of white women had worked the previous year compared to about 59 percent of black

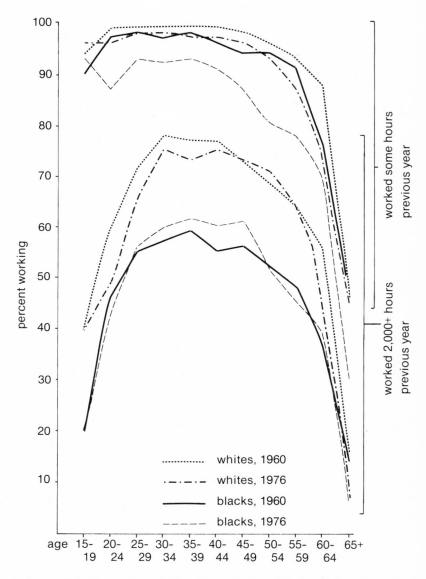

Figure 5.1. Proportion of Male Householders (Husbands and Other Male Heads) Who Worked Previous Year and Who Worked 2,000 or More Hours Previous Year, by Age and Race: 1960 and 1976.

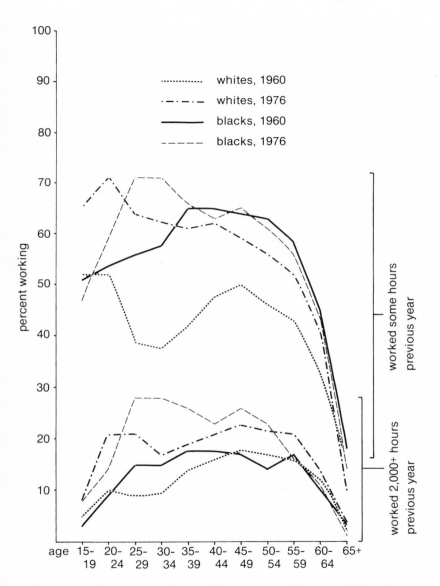

Figure 5.2. Proportion of Female Householders (Wives and Other Female Heads) Who Worked Previous Year and Who Worked 2,000 or More Hours Previous Year, by Age and Race: 1960 and 1976.

Table 5.1. *Proportion of Householders of Working Age (<65) Who Worked Previous Year and Who Worked Full Time Previous Year by Race, Sex, and Year*

	Sample *n*	Percent worked previous year	Percent worked full time
White males			
1960	33,796	97.0	70.8
1970	37,777	96.0	70.8
1976	26,421	93.6	66.7
Black males			
1960	3,006	94.3	53.1
1970	3,427	91.7	58.2
1976	2,324	86.3	53.4
White females			
1960	37,782	43.8	13.5
1970	42,424	54.4	17.2
1976	29,866	58.8	19.6
Black females			
1960	3,758	59.4	15.2
1970	4,622	62.6	17.6
1976	3,358	62.8	22.4

[a] Worked 2,000 or more hours. Hours estimate arrived at by multiplying hours worked in the week prior to the census times weeks worked previous year.

women, a differential of 15 percent. Although labor force participation rose among both races between 1960 and 1970, the increase was less for black women, so that the racial differential narrowed to only 9 percentage points in 1970. Rates for white women were higher still in 1976 (nearly 59 percent) while rates for black women (nearly 63 percent) were virtually unchanged, with the resulting racial differential down to 4 percentage points.

Labor Force Participation of Female Householders

Sweet (1973), among others, has shown that wives' labor force participation is quite responsive to the number of children and the age of the youngest child in a household. He also suggests that having a nonworking relative present, who can do housework and provide child care, is conducive to labor force participation. Many investigations (see Sweet, 1973; Bowen and Finegan, 1969; Waite, 1976; Cain, 1966) have shown that wives' participation is responsive to their husbands' incomes.

Bowen and Finegan (1969), in analyzing demographic correlates of labor force participation of women in different marital status and age categories in 1960, have demonstrated that labor force attachment is positively correlated with educational attainment and also that there is a strong age pattern of participation, due to the relation of age to family life cycle stage.

The 1960–1976 period was one of considerable change in the familial and economic roles of women. Because of the increase in wives' employment and the growth in female-headed families, the labor force participation of women became crucial to an ever larger number of households. My interest here is in whether the relationship between marital and family status and women's labor force participation changed between 1960 and 1976 and in whether relationships and changes were similar for white and black women. Table 5.2 presents a multiple classification analysis in which the dependent measure[2] is whether a female householder worked the previous year. Age, education, number of children in the household, whether the woman had an own child under six, whether a nonworking relative was present, and the level of income other than the woman's earnings are factors included in the model. Region (i.e., South vs. all other) and marital status (i.e., married spouse present, divorced, separated, widowed, never married) are also included.

Table 5.2. Multiple Classification Analysis of Employment for White and Black Female Householders[a]

	1960					
	White			Black		
		Deviations			Deviations	
	n	Gross	Net	n	Gross	Net
Age						
14–19	718	.081	.045	63	−.086	−.042
20–24	2990	.083	.143	325	−.059	.026
25–29	4142	−.044	.089	461	−.039	.027
30–34	4778	−.062	.062	542	−.019	.032
35–39	5245	−.014	.061	529	.054	.076
40–44	4960	.037	.043	533	.049	.035
45–49	4571	.064	−.002	446	.049	.049
50–54	4006	.022	−.086	355	.031	−.047
55–59	3446	−.055	−.148	302	−.011	−.103
60–64	2926	−.104	−.273	202	−.149	−.241
Education						
≤8	10218	−.083	−.095	1917	−.014	−.030
9–11	8259	.001	−.004	909	−.022	−.009
12	13061	.021	.030	607	−.024	.004
13–15	3880	.051	.066	195	.144	.166
16	1718	.104	.121	92	.221	.239
Over 16	646	.295	.235	38	.327	.265
Children						
None	14694	.105	.087	1345	.062	.023
1	7512	.030	.015	653	.034	.034
2	7475	−.069	−.075	531	−.010	−.003
3	4425	−.128	−.097	404	−.062	−.039
4	2134	−.155	−.094	295	−.035	.005
5	838	−.210	−.130	184	−.115	−.080
6 or more	704	−.247	−.137	346	−.123	−.064
Age youngest own child						
<6	12022	−.146	−.146	1299	−.103	−.096
Other	25760	.068	.068	2459	.054	.051

		1960				
		White			*Black*	
		Deviations			*Deviations*	
	n	*Gross*	*Net*	*n*	*Gross*	*Net*
Presence of non-working relative						
Present	2061	.092	.068	310	.057	.074
Not Present	35721	−.005	−.004	3448	−.005	−.007
Other income						
None	2175	.322	.125	418	.234	.169
1–2999	3969	.096	.041	946	.026	.030
3–5999	4615	.025	.047	933	−.015	−.001
6–8999	6752	.039	.062	728	−.075	−.063
9–11999	8003	−.023	.006	422	−.082	−.073
12–14999	5290	−.065	−.042	167	−.043	−.064
15 and over	6978	−.133	−.129	144	−.080	−.074
Region						
South	10228	−.009	−.018	2118	.023	.027
Other	27554	.003	.007	1640	−.030	−.035
Marital status						
Married, spouse present	32897	−.041	−.027	2727	−.046	−.022
Divorced	1772	.299	.189	537	.138	.061
Widowed	2023	.163	.151	358	.096	.086
Never married	1090	.455	.214	136	.119	−.020
Grand mean		.438			.594	
Adjusted R^2		.161			.091	

[a]MCA: Dependent variable = worked previous year/did not work previous year.

Table 5.2, continued

	1970					
	White			Black		
	Deviations			Deviations		
	n	*Gross*	*Net*	*n*	*Gross*	*Net*
Age						
14–19	715	.054	.036	98	−.136	−.117
20–24	4310	.013	.142	516	.029	.048
25–29	5033	−.021	.090	566	.021	.039
30–34	4540	−.057	.065	615	.044	.069
35–39	4606	−.022	.059	567	.044	.048
40–44	5098	.022	.040	540	.041	.037
45–49	5250	.030	−.010	500	.030	.012
50–54	4741	.028	−.058	489	−.031	−.055
55–59	4392	−.016	−.127	405	−.080	−.110
60–64	3739	−.130	−.262	326	−.169	−.184
Education						
≤8	7109	−.108	−.108	1410	−.107	−.093
9–11	8646	−.026	−.026	1414	−.022	−.023
12	17709	.016	.022	1248	.071	.069
13–15	5063	.043	.036	325	.097	.081
16	2675	.080	.077	131	.298	.257
Over 16	1220	.233	.181	94	.236	.186
Children						
None	18008	.078	.069	1540	.029	.034
1	7988	.033	.026	852	.023	.021
2	7759	−.066	−.070	767	.032	.013
3	4667	−.109	−.094	499	−.027	−.043
4	2405	−.136	−.106	398	−.025	−.019
5	963	−.167	−.121	280	−.094	−.077
6 or more	634	−.243	−.152	286	−.140	−.101
Age youngest own child						
<6	11037	−.137	−.154	1436	−.061	−.087
Other	31387	.048	.054	3186	.028	.039

	\multicolumn{6}{c}{1970}					
	\multicolumn{3}{c}{White}			\multicolumn{3}{c}{Black}	
	\multicolumn{3}{c}{Deviations}			\multicolumn{3}{c}{Deviations}	
	n	Gross	Net	n	Gross	Net
Presence of non-working relative						
Present	1794	.039	.041	296	−.031	.002
Not Present	40630	−.002	−.002	4326	.002	.000
Other income						
None	2638	.285	.124	614	.187	.178
1–2999	3584	.097	.034	815	−.039	−.002
3–5999	3896	.021	.020	889	−.084	−.064
6–8999	5096	.029	.051	782	−.025	−.034
9–11999	6481	.029	.050	657	.099	.000
12–14999	6634	−.018	.008	410	.023	−.007
15 and over	14092	−.099	−.082	455	−.024	−.047
Region						
South	12155	−.004	−.011	2278	.019	.040
Other	30269	.002	.005	2344	−.019	−.039
Marital status						
Married, spouse present	35705	−.041	−.026	2955	−.011	.010
Divorced	2671	.249	.166	905	.055	.004
Widowed	2520	.119	.125	443	−.062	−.037
Never married	1528	.329	.115	319	.029	−.054
Grand mean		.544			.626	
Adjusted R^2		.134			.095	

Table 5.2, continued

	1976					
	White			Black		
		Deviations			Deviations	
	n	Gross	Net	n	Gross	Net
Age						
14–19	533	.057	.049	53	−.156	−.119
20–24	3116	.122	.115	388	−.037	−.035
25–29	4234	.053	.111	503	.082	.050
30–34	3685	−.015	.071	409	.086	.082
35–39	3179	.021	.082	382	.030	.058
40–44	2979	.036	.051	370	.002	.019
45–49	3210	.006	−.023	340	.025	.022
50–54	3360	−.024	−.083	351	−.015	−.026
55–59	2964	−.070	−.151	307	−.064	−.075
60–64	2606	−.186	−.278	255	−.196	−.017
Education						
≤8	3600	−.173	−.154	727	−.152	−.124
9–11	4705	−.086	−.083	879	−.089	−.062
12	13793	.012	.017	1174	.070	.058
13–15	4239	.069	.054	348	.131	.094
16	2376	.124	.102	164	.251	.178
Over 16	1153	.236	.204	66	.297	.231
Children						
None	13277	.054	.053	1175	.021	.023
1	6017	.013	.012	725	.046	.031
2	5761	−.051	−.062	598	.033	.026
3	2905	−.080	−.075	368	−.062	−.067
4	1197	−.112	−.088	205	−.062	−.050
5	430	−.167	−.115	143	−.096	−.057
6 or more	279	−.226	−.144	144	−.197	−.157
Age youngest own child						
<6	7145	−.117	−.162	925	−.061	−.076
Other	22721	.037	.051	2433	.023	.029

	1976					
	White			Black		
	Deviations			Deviations		
	n	Gross	Net	*n*	Gross	Net
Presence of non-working relative						
Present	901	−.007	.039	177	.005	.047
Not Present	28965	.0002	−.001	3181	−.0003	−.003
Other income						
None	1091	.285	.182	355	.313	.312
1–2999	3276	.162	.119	774	−.031	.022
3–5999	3881	−.039	−.003	672	−.162	−.112
6–8999	3775	.004	.030	490	−.003	−.022
9–11999	4153	.027	.042	427	.014	−.036
12–14999	4051	−.012	−.006	283	.030	−.030
15 and over	10139	−.098	−.085	357	.022	−.050
Region						
South	9075	.011	.013	1684	.050	.064
Other	20791	−.005	−.006	1674	−.050	−.064
Marital status						
Married, spouse present	24359	−.034	−.011	1854	.008	.039
Divorced	2658	.156	.058	786	.012	−.033
Widowed	1511	.007	.043	322	−.109	−.066
Never married	1338	.299	.030	396	.027	−.064
Grand mean		.588			.627	
Adjusted R^2		.138			.092	

Among whites, married women were less likely to work than were other women, but net deviations by marital status declined considerably over the period. Whereas in 1960 the net deviations indicate almost a 20 percentage point difference in the labor force participation of married versus never-married women, by 1976 the spread between married and divorced women (i.e., those with the highest participation rates) was only around 7 percentage points.

For black women the employment picture by marital status was quite different from that of white women. In 1960 and 1970, net deviations among black women in different marital statuses were considerably smaller than the deviation among whites. Whereas in 1960 black married women were less likely to work than single, separated, or divorced women—as was true of whites—by 1976 married black women worked *more* often than women of any other marital status. This change is significant, since by 1976 a majority of working-age black women were in those other marital statuses (see Bianchi and Farley, 1979).

Having an own child under six deterred labor force participation for both races but the differential in participation rates between those who did and did not have a preschooler was greater for white women than for black women at each time point. The greater the number of children in the household, the less likely a female head was to work. This was true for both races, but, again, differentials among number of child categories were greater for white women than for black women.

In Figure 5.2, a very different age pattern of employment emerged for black and white female householders. Once other variables such as child–marital status are considered, however, the relationship between age and employment seems more similar for black and white women, particularly in the 1970s. Labor force participation rises at the younger ages and then tapers off for both races, although the rise is more slow for black women and the decline at older ages less substantial.

The influence of having a nonworking relative, a potential babysitter, present in the household was in the predictable direction but was not particularly strong at any time point. Finally, as has been noted elsewhere, educational attainment showed a strong, positive linear relation to labor force participation just as amount of other income showed a strong negative relation. This was true for both races and at each point in time.

Extent of Labor Force Participation of Female Householders

Some of the variation in the annual number of hours worked by women is a function of the same factors that affect whether or not they enter the labor force at all. That is, women's extent of participation is influenced, among other factors, by whether or not they have children, the number and age of children, their own level of education and labor force experience, the amount of other income in the household, whether or not there's a babysitter present, and their marital–household status (i.e., whether they are classified as "wife" or "other head"). It is unclear whether these factors influence black women in exactly the same way as white women, or whether these factors were of equal importance at each point in time.

Table 5.3 shows the variation in the annual number of hours worked by all female householders (i.e., wives and other female heads) who worked some hours the previous year. Means and standard deviations of variables used to predict hours worked are also presented. Hours are predicted by number of children, educational attainment, and marital status (i.e., married, spouse present, other), whether a child under six (a preschooler) is present in the household, whether a nonworking relative is present, and the amount of household income from sources other than the female householder's earnings.

Table 5.3. Means (Standard Deviations) of Variables in Hours and Earnings Equations of Female Householders

	1960		1970		1976	
	White	Black	White	Black	White	Black
Annual hours	1,371.05 (776.96)	1,243.90 (788.73)	1,434.20 (738.93)	1,428.20 (700.74)	1,391.51 (819.69)	1,435.69 (776.61)
Earnings[a]	$4,364.10 (3,486.96)	$2,610.74 (2,624.86)	$5,713.21 (4,885.24)	$4,769.77 (4,213.50)	$5,463.14 (4,361.88)	$5,212.84 (3,905.15)
Marital status (percentage married)	.781 (.413)	.662 (.473)	.775 (.418)	.627 (.484)	.762 (.426)	.560 (.497)
Presence of preschoolers (i.e., child < 6)	.225 (.418)	.352 (.478)	.207 (.405)	.337 (.473)	.200 (.400)	.308 (.462)
Number of children	1.041 (1.315)	1.716 (2.088)	1.082 (1.375)	1.774 (1.935)	1.008 (1.262)	1.498 (1.650)
Years of potential labor market employment	23.42 (12.91)	25.04 (12.78)	22.74 (13.56)	22.56 (13.31)	20.64 (13.36)	21.18 (13.36)

	1960		1970		1976	
	White	Black	White	Black	White	Black
Years^2	714.93	790.11	700.94	686.13	604.49	627.05
	(639.87)	(695.77)	(646.90)	(677.14)	(616.58)	(688.72)
Education	11.06	8.80	11.68	10.43	12.31	11.34
	(2.92)	(3.66)	(2.76)	(3.21)	(2.59)	(2.93)
Occupation SEI	38.26	18.78	40.96	27.43	43.29	31.30
	(20.31)	(17.02)	(20.97)	(21.40)	(20.25)	(21.57)
Presence of nonworking relative	.0665	.0902	.0452	.0611	.0293	.0533
	(.249)	(.287)	(.208)	(.240)	(.169)	(.225)
Other income[a]	$8,552.23	$5,003.09	$11,499.22	$6,933.80	$11,335.96	$6,736.74
	(6,791.22)	(5,103.80)	(10,120.54)	(6,551.71)	(9,471.09)	(6,434.52)
Region (South)	.261	.576	.284	.507	.310	.535
	(.439)	(.494)	(.451)	(.500)	(.463)	(.499)

[a] Expressed in 1975 dollars.

Rather than age per se, a measure of "potential labor force employment" (age minus years of school minus six) is used. This variable and its square are widely used proxies for labor force experience (see Mincer, 1976). If skills build over time, it is conceivable that with experience workers will be less subject to layoffs or underemployment. But as workers age there are a host of factors operating to decrease their extent of employment—hence the squared term. Skills become outdated so that persons who have worked one job a long time may be increasingly likely to suffer unemployment and underemployment. Health factors may decrease the extent of employment of older workers. As seniority increases, those who have worked a number of years may be able to receive pensions, qualify for early retirement, or reduce to part time their employment. These proxies for labor market experience are best for full-time workers and for workers who have had a continuous attachment to the labor force. Because women's labor force experience tends to be discontinuous over the life cycle, and because women often work part time, these measures are not particularly good indicators of time spent in the labor force. However, they represent the best approximations available with these data.

Table 5.4 presents the regression coefficients for equations predicting the annual number of hours of labor market participation for black and white female householders. Although number of children and having a preschool child in the household have the expected negative effects on hours of labor market participation for both races, children as a "depressant" on hours of employment are much more significant at each point for white women than for black. Hence, among blacks, not only is entry into the labor force less responsive to the presence of children than for whites, but also the number of hours worked is less influenced by children than for whites.

If a woman was living with a spouse in 1960, she was likely

to work fewer hours than if she was a female heading a household without a spouse present. This remained true for whites in 1970 and 1976, but among blacks this was less true in 1970 than in 1960 and not at all the case in 1976. Having a relative present to babysit/do housework did seem to encourage greater labor force employment—more so in 1970 than in 1960 and more so in 1976 than in 1970.

Hours of employment increased more with years since school (i.e., years of potential employment) for white women than for black in 1960, but since that time, coefficients are quite similar for both races. Relative to other factors, the experience variables are the most important to the regression for each time point and for each race (see standardized coefficients in Table 5.4). Regression coefficients for education were larger for black than for white women and were highest for 1976, suggesting that an additional year of schooling led to greater increases in hours worked for black than for white women, net of other variables. And, among both races, an additional year of schooling in 1976 yielded a greater increase in hours of employment than in 1960 and 1970. Finally, the amount of other income influenced white female householders' hours of employment but had no detectable influence on black women's extent of employment.

In sum, black and white women differed at each point in the proportion employed but in the 1970s differed hardly at all in the average annual hours worked when they were employed (see Table 5.3). Family status variables, particularly number of children and age of youngest child, were more influential in determining the number of hours and probability of employment of white female than of black female householders. The data also show a racial difference in employment by marital–headship status. White wives consistently at each point had lower levels of employment and worked fewer hours than those white women who headed their own households. While this was true

Table 5.4. Prediction of Annual Hours Worked Previous Year by Black and White Female Householders (Wives and Other Heads)

	Number of children	Preschooler present	Years potential employment	(Years)^2	Education
	Metric coefficients[a]				
1960					
White	−96.17	−260.71	29.15	−0.55	11.75
	(5.69)	(18.21)	(1.80)	(.04)	(2.26)
Black	−19.86	−147.36	12.63	−0.22	26.98
	(10.54)	(47.52)	(5.33)	(.101)	(5.56)
1970					
White	−85.62	−212.06	27.03	−.52	7.68
	(4.25)	(14.08)	(1.42)	(.03)	(1.92)
Black	−31.42	−82.65	26.84	−.50	33.43
	(8.12)	(33.69)	(3.88)	(.08)	(4.95)
1976					
White	−101.35	−268.59	33.50	−.66	38.96
	(5.91)	(17.48)	(1.92)	(.04)	(2.59)
Black	−47.01	−84.87	34.12	−.61	67.82
	(11.87)	(41.34)	(5.02)	(.10)	(7.11)
	Standardized coefficients				
1960					
White	−.163	−.140	.484	−.456	.044
Black	.053	.089	.205	−.194	.125
1970					
White	−.159	−.116	.496	−.455	.029
Black	−.087	−.056	.510	−.483	.153
1976					
White	−.156	−.141	.546	−.499	.123
Black	−.100	−.050	.587	−.522	.256

[a]Standard errors are in parentheses and are based on the assumption of simple random sampling. For the 1976 CPS estimates, standard errors of the regression coefficients should be inflated by 10 percent in

Presence of babysitter	Other income	Married	Constant	R^2	Sample n
		Metric coefficients[a]			
116.20 (23.25)	−.010 (.001)	−203.28 (16.74)	1,349.82	.136	15,825
70.00 (58.17)	.004 (.015)	−283.83 (38.75)	1,119.88	.065	2,162
140.26 (22.50)	−.006 (.001)	−192.66 (12.94)	1,447.72	.109	22,618
114.98 (53.28)	.0002 (.002)	−126.27 (31.29)	970.87	.066	2,863
144.07 (35.16)	−.010 (.0008)	−184.40 (16.81)	1,026.73	.122	17,116
166.58 (71.94)	−.006 (.003)	−7.22 (40.82)	454.14	.100	2,161
		Standardized coefficients			
.037	−.088	−.108			
.025	−.015	−.170			
.039	−.088	−.109			
.039	.002	−.087			
.030	−.115	−.096			
.048	−.005	−.005			

order to take into account the design effect for the multistage, cluster sampling design (see Frankel, 1971:116).

of black women in 1960, by 1976 black wives were more likely than other female heads to be employed and there was no differential in hours worked by marital–headship status.

Extent of Labor Force Participation of Male Householders

As was shown in Table 5.1, although almost all black and white male heads worked at each time point, only 65–70 percent of white males and 53–58 percent of black males worked an estimated 2,000 or more hours. The racial differential in number of hours worked was much more substantial than the differential in percent who worked at all.

Researchers have suggested that blacks fare best in a tight labor market (Harrison, 1972) and are hard hit by unemployment and underemployment in times of recession, such as those of the 1970s. Unfortunately, these data do not contain sufficient indicators of labor market conditions to explore this suggestion, but information on several individual or household characteristics that may be important determinants of racial differences in employment are available.

Bowen and Finegan (1969), in assessing predictors of labor force participation rates of males in 1960, found that marital status was a strong predictor. Other determinants of labor force participation rates included educational attainment and age. In addition, whether presence and number of children are related to the time men spend in the labor force is investigated in this analysis. Like marital status, child–family status variables might be assumed to influence participation since these constitute added economic demands placed on a particular household.

Black and white men differ in marital–family status distributions. They differ in educational and age (or experience) distributions. Also, given changes over the 1960–1976 period, the marital–family status distributions of male household heads of both races have changed. More households are other than husband and wife, and in husband–wife households, the proportion containing children has declined.

Table 5.5 presents means and standard deviations of variables used to predict annual hours worked the previous year. Hours are predicted by marital–headship status (i.e., married spouse present vs. all other), whether or not there are children under 18 in the household and the number of children, years of schooling and "potential years of employment" (age minus years of school minus six) and its square.

Table 5.6 presents regression results for black and white male heads of households at each point in time. The dependent variable is annual hours worked the previous year. The analysis is restricted to those male householders, under 65, who worked some hours the previous year and who had some earnings in that year. At each point, black males averaged 2–300 fewer hours of work than white males.

For both races, men who were married and who had children worked more hours than childless, unmarried men. Having or not having children was the important factor; number of children seemed not to influence the number of hours a male householder worked. Both years of potential labor market activity and educational attainment were related to hours of employment for both races and at each time point. Coefficients were of greater magnitude in 1976 than in 1960 and somewhat larger for whites.

Perhaps the most important conclusion to be drawn from this analysis is that very little of the variation in employment can be explained by individual and household characteristics. Only 3 to 7 percent of the variation in annual hours worked is ever explained by marital–child status, educational attainment, and potential years in the labor force (see R^2 in Table 5.6).

Studies that attempt to incorporate labor market condi-

Table 5.5. Means (Standard Deviations) of Variables in Hours and Earnings Equations of Male Householders

	1960		1970		1976	
	White	Black	White	Black	White	Black
Annual hours	2,120.71	1,838.18	2,122.86	1,951.91	2,087.38	1,835.22
	(623.87)	(690.97)	(591.42)	(562.19)	(772.09)	(740.34)
Earnings[a]	$10,303.83	$5,640.80	$13,823.94	$8,649.14	$13,520.28	$8,971.31
	(6,467.20)	(3,925.72)	(9,299.04)	(5,235.30)	(9,980.46)	(5,156.54)
Marital status	.931	.870	.907	.830	.881	.776
(percentage married)	(.254)	(.337)	(.291)	(.376)	(.324)	(.417)
Presence of children	.653	.630	.608	.628	.567	.581
	(.476)	(.483)	(.488)	(.483)	(.495)	(.494)
Number of children	1.516	1.981	1.407	1.807	1.199	1.406
	(1.554)	(2.272)	(1.539)	(2.083)	(1.366)	(1.700)

	1960		1970		1976	
	White	Black	White	Black	White	Black
Years of potential labor market employment	25.24 (12.80)	27.31 (13.02)	24.06 (13.29)	25.68 (13.95)	22.17 (13.17)	23.76 (13.91)
Years^2	801.17 (688.61)	915.29 (752.76)	755.46 (676.62)	854.03 (767.31)	664.98 (641.04)	757.78 (739.80)
Education	10.65 (3.47)	7.83 (3.93)	11.67 (3.33)	9.48 (3.69)	12.43 (3.11)	10.58 (3.54)
Occupation SEI	36.14 (22.27)	18.44 (15.36)	40.51 (23.74)	24.78 (18.70)	42.23 (24.07)	27.60 (19.99)
Region (South)	.265 (.441)	.570 (.495)	.279 (.449)	.492 (.500)	.301 (.459)	.508 (.500)

[a]Expressed in 1975 dollars.

Table 5.6. Prediction of Annual Hours Worked Previous Year by Black and White Male Householders (Husbands and Other Heads)

	Presence of children	Number of children	Years potential employment	$(Years)^2$	Education
	Metric coefficients[a]				
1960					
White	70.70	6.49	19.22	−.36	23.94
	(10.85)	(3.16)	(1.08)	(.02)	(1.15)
Black	44.16	−2.09	14.67	−.25	17.91
	(38.37)	(7.79)	(4.24)	(.07)	(4.05)
1970					
White	82.35	3.93	31.12	−.60	11.15
	(9.69)	(2.95)	(.91)	(.02)	(1.05)
Black	108.42	−10.93	17.91	−.28	17.81
	(29.46)	(6.53)	(2.92)	(.05)	(3.41)
1976					
White	50.57	1.16	33.06	−.65	38.09
	(16.02)	(5.57)	(1.54)	(.03)	(1.74)
Black	104.91	−9.61	24.28	−.39	30.57
	(49.76)	(13.62)	(4.66)	(.09)	(5.84)
	Standardized coefficients				
1960					
White	.054	.016	.395	−.393	.133
Black	.031	−.007	.276	−.277	.102
1970					
White	.068	.010	.700	−.684	.063
Black	.093	−.040	.444	−.385	.117
1976					
White	.032	.002	.564	−.538	.154
Black	.070	−.022	.456	−.389	.146

[a] Standard errors are in parentheses and are based on the assumption of simple random sampling. For the 1976 CPS estimates, standard errors of the regression coefficients should be inflated by 10 percent in

	Married spouse present	Constant	R^2	Sample n
		Metric coefficients[a]		
1960				
White	193.01 (14.12)	1,430.79	.047	32,117
Black	159.40 (41.64)	1,367.55	.024	2,811
1970				
White	169.82 (11.02)	1,486.24	.066	35,871
Black	120.42 (28.69)	1,415.73	.036	3,141
1976				
White	119.00 (16.29)	1,176.94	.054	24,493
Black	143.68 (44.17)	1,071.22	.045	2,069
		Standardized coefficients		
1960				
White	.078			
Black	.078			
1970				
White	.084			
Black	.080			
1976				
White	.050			
Black	.081			

order to take into account the design effect for the multistage, cluster sampling design (see Frankel, 1971:116).

tions into the analysis of racial differentials in employment have also been unable to adequately explain the black–white differential in employment. For example, Kain (1968) has argued that blacks miss out on employment opportunities because they are segregated in the housing market; but when Masters (1975: 91–94) investigated the relative employment rates of black and white men for a subsample of SMSA's in 1970, he found only modest support for the Kain explanation of differential employment rates.

It is likely that an important explanatory factor in the racial differential in annual hours worked is that blacks have differential access to information about jobs and to networks leading to stable, full–time/full-year employment. Field observation, such as that of Liebow (1967), suggests the importance of such factors. It may be the case that residence patterns have the effect of limiting job opportunities, but that aggregate measurement at the SMSA level has been too gross to capture these effects. In any event, much further investigation of racial differentials in employment is needed.

Hours, Implied Wages, and Earnings of Householders

Table 5.7 reports the mean earnings, hours, and implied wage rates (i.e., earnings/hours) for nonelderly male and female heads who had earnings at each time point. All figures have been converted to 1975 dollars. Figures are reported for all black and white male and female householders and for husbands, wives, other male and female heads separately. Estimates suggest improvements over time in the wage rates of total male and female householders of each race. The only instance where the pattern of improvement does not hold is in the wage rates of black and white other female heads, 1970–1976. Estimates of mean implied wages in 1976 were somewhat lower than 1970 estimates. This is a significant statistic since these are the women most likely to be providing total support for themselves and dependent children.

Racial differentials shown in Table 5.7 are substantial, particularly for males. In addition, differentials by sex are extremely large and have remained so throughout the period. Although the ratio of black to white implied wage rates increased from 68 percent to 77 percent for males and from 71 to 84 percent for females, ratios of female to male wages changed little for either race between 1960 and 1976. On average, the implied wage rate of white females was only 69 percent that of white males in 1976; wages of black females were 75 percent those of black males and only 58 percent those of white males.

Race and sex earnings disparities were even greater than implied wage rate disparities, due partially to differentials in the number of hours worked by each group. Black and white male and female heads also differ on several characteristics that are known to influence earnings levels. These determinants of race and sex differentials in earnings are investigated in the next section.

Earnings of Householders

Table 5.8 presents regression coefficients for equations predicting annual earnings of black and white, male and female householders who had earnings in the previous year. Earnings are predicted by education (years of schooling), occupational status (Duncan SEI codes),[3] years of potential employment (age minus years of school minus six) and years of potential employment squared, annual hours worked the previous year (hours worked the week of the survey times weeks worked the previous year), region (South coded 1, otherwise 0), and marital status (married spouse present coded 1, otherwise 0).[4] Marital

Table 5.7. *Mean Earnings, Annual Hours Worked, and Implied Wage Rates of Householders by Race, Sex, Marital Status, and Year*

	1960			1970			1976		
	Males	Females	Ratio (F/M)	Males	Females	Ratio (F/M)	Males	Females	Ratio (F/M)
				All household heads					
Earnings[a]									
Whites	$10,304	$4,364	.42	$13,824	$5,713	.41	$13,520	$5,463	.40
Blacks	5,641	2,611	.46	8,649	4,770	.55	8,971	5,213	.58
Ratio (B/W)	.54	.60		.63	.83		.66	.95	
Hours									
Whites	2,121	1,371	.64	2,123	1,434	.68	2,087	1,392	.67
Blacks	1,838	1,244	.68	1,952	1,428	.73	1,835	1,436	.78
Ratio (B/W)	.87	.91		.92	1.00		.88	1.03	
Wage[b]									
Whites	$5.29	$3.84	.73	$7.06	$4.52	.64	$7.26	$5.00	.69
Blacks	3.59	2.74	.76	4.85	4.09	.84	5.61	4.19	.75
Ratio (B/W)	.68	.71		.69	.90		.77	.84	

	1960			1970			1976		
	Males	Females	Ratio (F/M)	Males	Females	Ratio (F/M)	Males	Females	Ratio (F/M)
				Husbands/wives					
Earnings[a]									
Whites	$10,445	$3,984	.38	$14,107	$5,186	.37	$13,870	$5,021	.36
Blacks	5,720	2,443	.43	8,826	4,573	.52	9,247	5,108	.55
Ratio (B/W)	.55	.61		.63	.88		.67	1.02	
Hours									
Whites	2,140	1,285	.60	2,147	1,358	.63	2,109	1,305	.62
Blacks	1,864	1,147	.62	1,979	1,377	.70	1,880	1,418	.75
Ratio (B/W)	.87	.89		.92	1.01		.89	1.09	
Wage[b]									
Whites	$5.30	$3.80	.72	$7.12	$4.35	.61	$7.34	$5.07	.69
Blacks	3.55	2.88	.81	4.90	3.94	.80	5.53	4.23	.76
Ratio (B/W)	.67	.76		.69	.91		.75	.83	

Table 5.7, continued

	1960			1970			1976		
	Males	Females	Ratio (F/M)	Males	Females	Ratio (F/M)	Males	Females	Ratio (F/M)
				Other heads					
Earnings[a]									
Whites	$8,402	$5,723	.68	$11,075	$7,527	.68	$10,938	$6,879	.63
Blacks	5,109	2,940	.58	7,786	5,100	.66	8,014	5,346	.67
Ratio (B/W)	.61	.52		.70	.68		.74	.78	
Hours									
Whites	1,878	1,679	.89	1,893	1,696	.90	1,926	1,668	.87
Blacks	1,669	1,433	.86	1,818	1,515	.83	1,679	1,459	.87
Ratio (B/W)	.89	.85		.96	.89		.87	.87	
Wage[b]									
Whites	$5.21	$3.99	.77	$6.52	$5.12	.79	$6.64	$4.76	.72
Blacks	3.87	2.47	.64	4.60	4.33	.94	5.87	4.14	.71
Ratio (B/W)	.74	.62		.71	.85		.88	.87	

[a]Expressed in 1975 dollars.
[b]Earnings divided by annual hours.

status is included because the foregoing analysis suggests that it may stand for a set of pressures/choices that influence both the type and extent of employment and hence the wage rates at which heads seek employment.

As can be seen in the same table, white women's earnings were considerably less if they were wives than if they were other heads at each time point. Black women's earnings were less different by marital status, although wives in general earned less than other heads, even after other variables were taken into account.

Over time, the racial differential in average return to hours of employment has narrowed considerably for females. By 1976 black and white women had quite comparable returns to education, occupation, years of potential employment, and hours of market activity. Living in the South, however, remained a greater disadvantage to black women than to white women.

Table 5.8 also shows that black males averaged substantially lower returns for educational attainment, occupational status, and years of potential employment than did white males. Contrary to the situation for females, there has been no great narrowing of the differences in returns to education, occupation, and experience for males. If anything, the 1976 differentials were larger than in 1960 and 1970. As with black women, living in the South appears to have been more disadvantageous to black males than to whites at each point.

Even after other differences are taken into account, particularly hours of labor market participation, both black and white husbands earned more at each point than other male heads. Perhaps not surprisingly, this is just the reverse of the situation for women. Whether there really is something about being married that is economically advantageous to men and disadvantageous to women or a host of unmeasured variables associated with marital status are acting to produce this relation, it is interesting that the relationship holds at each point. Relative

Table 5.8. Prediction of Earnings of Male and Female Householders

	Education	Occupation	Years potential employment	Years²	Region (South)	Marital status	Annual hours	Constant	R²	Sample n
Metric coefficients[a]										
Data for males										
1960										
White	410.34 (12.40)	82.63 (1.69)	337.85 (9.66)	-5.34 (.180)	-1,259.02 (70.38)	1,287.55 (122.32)	1.72 (.051)	-5,820.01	.276	32,117
Black	202.15 (22.00)	50.47 (4.61)	144.68 (20.38)	-2.23 (.348)	-2,203.94 (131.17)	388.42 (186.77)	1.27 (.092)	-202.94	.294	2,811
1970										
White	584.83 (17.68)	101.65 (2.22)	509.68 (12.50)	-8.11 (.247)	-1,410.50 (95.27)	1,784.14 (147.46)	2.57 (.074)	-9,925.58	.255	35,871
Black	340.32 (29.60)	62.52 (4.76)	191.77 (22.85)	-2.69 (.418)	-2,256.20 (161.17)	934.75 (208.77)	2.17 (.140)	-2,662.31	.312	3,141
1976										
White	737.91 (24.32)	94.09 (2.88)	547.68 (16.49)	-8.74 (.340)	-917.75 (118.57)	1,478.92 (169.90)	2.59 (.072)	-12,397.82	.282	24,493
Black	296.69 (37.90)	49.35 (5.45)	207.86 (26.41)	-2.87 (.505)	-1,805.62 (191.34)	819.12 (222.80)	2.42 (.128)	-2,460.93	.347	2,069

	Education	Occupation	Years potential employment	Years²	Region (South)	Marital status	Annual hours	Constant	R²	Sample n
				Standardized coefficients						
1960										
White	.220	.285	.669	−.569	−.086	.050	.166			
Black	.203	.197	.480	−.428	−.278	.033	.224			
1970										
White	.209	.260	.728	−.590	−.068	.056	.163			
Black	.240	.223	.511	−.394	−.215	.067	.233			
1976										
White	.230	.227	.723	−.561	−.042	.048	.201			
Black	.204	.191	.561	−.411	−.175	.066	.348			

Table 5.8, continued

	Education	Occupation	Years potential employment	Years²	Region (South)	Marital status	Annual hours	Constant	R²	Sample n
Data for females				Metric coefficients[b]						
1960										
White	227.03 (9.35)	26.90 (1.24)	59.44 (5.83)	.714 (.119)	-574.00 (47.05)	-615.00 (52.55)	2.42 (.028)	-2,744.28	.450	15,825
Black	102.07 (16.04)	51.48 (2.96)	49.56 (12.73)	-.759 (.233)	-1,114.23 (84.69)	-161.82 (90.38)	1.30 (.053)	-762.66	.481	2,162
1970										
White	204.87 (12.35)	38.32 (1.52)	74.83 (7.15)	-.907 (.151)	-551.00 (58.51)	-1,131.92 (65.18)	3.01 (.037)	-3,767.99	.351	22,618
Black	300.33 (26.72)	60.75 (3.55)	71.33 (17.40)	-.740 (.346)	-974.16 (125.18)	-418.90 (128.38)	1.96 (.090)	-3,181.50	.398	2,863
1976										
White	294.59 (12.34)	36.62 (1.50)	66.89 (6.99)	-.862 (.152)	-347.47 (53.57)	-731.98 (59.59)	2.82 (.032)	-3,873.50	.454	17,116
Black	270.98 (28.04)	46.37 (3.35)	66.27 (16.17)	-.836 (.329)	-1,153.46 (115.67)	-271.74 (114.18)	2.46 (.077)	-2,949.06	.550	2,161

	Education	Occupation	Years potential employment	Years²	Region (South)	Marital status	Annual hours	Constant	R²	Sample n
				Standardized coefficients						
1960										
White	.190	.157	.220	−.131	−.072	−.073	.539			
Black	.142	.333	.241	−.201	−.210	−.029	.390			
1970										
White	.172	.165	.208	−.120	−.051	−.097	.455			
Black	.229	.309	.225	−.119	−.116	−.048	.327			
1976										
White	.175	.170	.205	−.122	−.037	−.072	.531			
Black	.203	.256	.227	−.143	−.147	−.035	.489			

[a]Standard errors are in parentheses and are based on the assumption of simple random sampling. For the 1976 CPS estimates, standard errors of the regression coefficients should be inflated by 10 percent in order to take into account the design effect for the multistage, cluster sampling design (see Frankel, 1971:116).

to other factors, however, marital status is one of the least influential predictors (see standardized coefficients at the bottom of Table 5.8).

Race and Sex Inequality, 1960–1976

There are substantial race and sex differences and also sizable improvements over time in the earnings of householders. Blacks and whites, men and women, differ not only in average characteristics but also in the rates of return to characteristics such as education and years in the labor force. There have also been changes over time in each of these components. It proves advantageous to break down average earnings differences between groups (and changes over time in average earnings of each group) into various components.

The decomposition is accomplished by means of the following equation:

$$[\bar{E}_1 - \bar{E}_2] = [b_{0_1} - b_{0_2}] + [\sum_{i=1}^{n} b_{i_2} (\bar{X}_{i_1} - \bar{X}_{i_2})]$$

$$\begin{bmatrix} \text{Difference in Average} \\ \text{Earnings between} \\ \text{group 1 or 2} \end{bmatrix} = \begin{bmatrix} \text{Intercept} \\ \text{Component} \end{bmatrix} + \begin{bmatrix} \text{Compositional} \\ \text{(Mean)} \\ \text{Component} \end{bmatrix}$$

$$+ \quad [\sum_{i=1}^{n} \bar{X}_{i_2} (b_{i_1} - b_{i_2})] \quad + \quad [\sum_{i=1}^{n} (b_{i_1} - b_{i_2}) (\bar{X}_{i_1} - \bar{X}_{i_2})]$$

$$+ \quad \begin{bmatrix} \text{Rate of Return} \\ \text{(Slope)} \\ \text{Component} \end{bmatrix} \quad + \quad [\text{Interaction Component}]$$

where group 1 and 2 are either two different race or sex groups or the same group at two points in time. The compositional differences are weighted by one group's regression coefficients just as rate differences are weighted by the same group's mean characteristics. In Table 5.9, the regression coefficients and mean characteristics of blacks (or white females) are used as the weights. Use of white males (cf. O. D. Duncan, 1969) would result in a slightly higher estimate of the compositional (mean) component. Blacks and women are used as a standard because most of the Equal Employment Opportunity (EEO) legislation has been aimed at equalizing or "bring blacks and women up to" the level of white men (Burstein, 1979). One might look at this decomposition as answering the questions: "What if black male and female householders had the same average level of education, occupational status, years in the labor force, worked the same number of hours, and were distributed across household type and by region as were white males? How much higher would their earnings have been at each point? On the other hand, what if black men and women retained their own average characteristics but had rates of return similar to white men? How much would earnings have been increased in 1960 and in 1976?"

Two comments about the decomposition are in order. First, one must keep in mind the hypothetical nature of these estimates. They provide a vehicle for quantifying and discussing potential gains but are not absolute. Different specification of the earnings model or use of a different decomposition technique can lead to somewhat different results (cf. Farley, 1979).

The second point has to do with the interpretation of the different components. Althauser and Wigler (1972) argue that the intercept component should be separated out from the rate of return (slope) component. In discussion of racial inequality, some researchers (e.g., Winsborough and Dickinson, 1971) have combined these two components while others (e.g., O. D. Duncan, 1969) have combined slope, intercept, and interaction components. Researchers have usually referred to the intercept plus rates (plus interaction) combination as a measure of discrimination. The fallacy of this interpretation is that other factors besides discrimination enter into slope differences, and mean dif-

Table 5.9. Decomposition of Earnings Gap between White Male Householders and All Other Groups[a]

| | 1960 | | | | | |
| | White females | | Black males | | Black females | |
	$	%	$	%	$	%
Average earnings[b]						
White males	$10,304		$10,304		$10,304	
Black males/						
females	4,364		5,641		2,611	
Difference	5,940		4,663		7,693	
Due to intercept						
+ rate (slope)						
differences	$4,644	78%	$1,183	26%	$3,222	42%
Due to intercept						
differences	−3,076	−52	−5,617	−120	−2,636	−34
Due to rate of						
return (slope)						
differences	7,720	130	6,800	146	5,858	76
Due to composi-						
tional (mean)						
differences	1,616	27	2,473	53	2,550	33
Due to interaction	−328	−5	1,005	20	2,047	26

[a] Data for black males/females are used as the standard for this decomposition. Decomposition is based on the following equation (WM = white males; OG = other race-sex groups)

	1976					
	White females		*Black males*		*Black females*	
	$	%	$	%	$	%
Average earnings[b]						
White males	$13,520		$13,520		$13,520	
Black males/						
females	5,463		8,971		5,213	
Difference	8,057		4,549		8,307	
Due to intercept						
+ rate (slope)						
differences	$5,770	72%	$867	19%	$3,837	46%
Due to intercept						
differences	−8,524	−106	−9,937	−218	−9,449	−114
Due to rate of						
return (slope)						
differences	14,294	177	10,804	237	13,322	160
Due to composi-						
tional (mean)						
differences	1,919	24	2,277	50	2,622	32
Due to interaction	359	5	1,404	31	1,799	22

$$\overline{E}_{WM} - \overline{E}_{OG} = [b_{0_{WM}} - b_{0_{OG}}] + [\sum_{i=1}^{n} \overline{X}_{i_{OG}}(b_{i_{WM}} - b_{i_{OG}})] + [\sum_{i=1}^{n} b_{i_{OG}}(\overline{X}_{i_{WM}} - \overline{X}_{i_{OG}})] + [\sum_{i=1}^{n} (b_{i_{WM}} - b_{i_{OG}})(\overline{X}_{i_{WM}} - \overline{X}_{i_{OG}})].$$

[b]Expressed in 1975 dollars.

Table 5.10. Decomposition of 1960–1976 Earnings Improvement of Householders[a]

	White males (husbands/ other)		White females (wives/other)	
	$	%	$	%
Average earnings, 1976[b]	$13,520		$5,463	
Average earnings, 1960[b]	10,304		4,364	
1960–1976 change	3,216	100%	1,099	100%
Due to intercept + rate (slope) differences	2,011	63	575	52
Due to intercept differences	−6,578	−205	−1,129	−103
Due to rate of return (slope) differences	8,589	267	1,704	155
Due to compositional (mean) differences	757	24	366	33
Due to interaction	445	14	150	14

[a]The 1960 data are used as the standard for this decomposition. Decomposition is based on the following equation. For each race-sex group,

ferences themselves result in part from discrimination. Rather than label one or the other component "discrimination," the purpose here is to assess the relative magnitude of the various components. No substantive interpretation of the large, negative intercept difference is afforded, and, following Winsborough and Dickinson, it is combined with slope differences.

As can be seen in Table 5.9, for male householders the average racial earnings differential narrowed slightly from about

	Black males (husbands/ other)		Black females (wives/other)	
	$	%	$	%
Average earnings, 1976[b]	$8,971		$5,213	
Average earnings, 1960[b]	5,641		2,611	
1960–1976 change	3,330	100%	2,602	100%
Due to intercept + rate (slope) differences	2,317	69	946	36
Due to intercept differences	−2,258	−68	−2,186	−84
Due to rate of return (slope) differences	4,675	137	3,135	120
Due to compositional (mean) differences	952	29	1,056	41
Due to interaction	107	3	572	22

$$\overline{E}_{76} - \overline{E}_{60} = b_{0_{76}} - b_{0_{60}} + \sum_{i=1}^{n} \overline{X}_{i_{60}}(b_{i_{76}} - b_{i_{60}}) + \sum_{i=1}^{n} b_{i_{60}}(\overline{X}_{i_{76}} - \overline{X}_{i_{60}}) +$$
$$\sum_{1}(b_{i_{76}} - b_{i_{60}})(\overline{X}_{i_{76}} - \overline{X}_{i_{60}}).$$

[b]Expressed in 1975 dollars.

$4,700 in 1960 to about $4,500 in 1976. Half of the $4,500 earnings differential could be apportioned to compositional differences between the races and an additional 30 percent resulted from the interaction of racial differences in average characteristics and dollar returns to those characteristics. On the other hand, about 20% of the racial differential could only be attributed to the lower dollar returns that black males received for characteristics similar to those of white males.

Whereas half of the $4,500 average earnings differential between white and black men could be apportioned to compositional differences between the races, only a third of the much larger $8,300 average earnings difference between black women and white men could be attributed to mean differences in hours worked, experience, education, occupation, marital status, and regional location. Almost half of the differential between black women and white men resulted from differential dollar returns to similar characteristics.

As noted by Burstein (1979), it is the earnings gap between white males and white females that has increased substantially in recent decades. Table 5.9 indicates that the average earnings differential between white male and female householders increased, approximately from $5,900 in 1960 to $8,000 in 1976. In addition, because white men and women are quite similar in average characteristics such as education attainment, only a quarter of the $8,000 difference between white males and females could be attributed to compositional differences. Most of this was due to the fewer hours worked per year by white women as compared with white men. Over 70 percent of the differential between white men and women could only be attributed to differences in dollar returns to similar characteristics.

In Table 5.10, I attempt to specify components of the changes over time in the earnings of male and female, black and white, householders. Average earnings gains by white females were least substantial ($1,100 on average) while those for males were most substantial (about $3,200 for white males and $3,300 for black males). Gains for black females were intermediate (just over $2,600) and brought 1976 average earnings of black women almost up to that of white women. Compositional shifts over the period, particularly the upgrading of the educational and occupational level of workers, were of importance for all groups, accounting for a quarter of the improvement for white men and as much as 41 percent of the improvement of black women. Around 30 percent of the improvement for white women and black men was attributable to upgrading of average characteristics.

In sum, although the 1960–1976 period was one of improvement for all, men fared better than women and the most advantaged group at the start of the period, white males, maintained a sizable earnings advantage over each of the other groups throughout the 1960s and 1970s.

Chapter 6

Economic Well-Being of Blacks and Whites

In Chapters 3 through 5, I have presented findings demonstrating that many changes occurred in black and white households between 1960 and 1976. Two types of households grew rapidly: persons living alone and female-headed families with dependent children. The growth in one-person units contributed to a reduction in average household size, as did the decline in fertility within marriage and the increase in divorce (which split one larger household into two smaller ones). The increase in divorce, however, also had the effect of separating a male wage earner from his children, and by the 1970s, the ratio of dependent children to available household earners was very high in female-headed families.

Within husband–wife, male- and female-headed households, racial differences in average household size declined, but, in 1976, black households remained considerably larger than similar white households. Dissimilarity in the black–white distributions across household type increased during the period because the growth in female-headed families with children was more substantial among blacks than among whites.

As husband–wife households became increasingly reliant upon both the wife's and husband's earnings, female-headed households came to rely either solely on the female head's earnings or on income from sources other than earnings. Among both races, differences in dependency ratios, income sources, and household labor force activity widened between husband–

wife and female-headed households. While labor force participation rates increased dramatically among wives, particularly
white wives, participation rates among other female heads did
not change much for whites and actually decreased among
blacks.

Throughout the period, it remained a distinct economic
advantage for a household to have a white, male wage earner
present. Analysis of earnings of nonelderly husbands, wives,
other female and male heads showed that, whereas all race–sex
groups witnessed real earnings improvements and black females largely caught-up to white females, dollar improvements
were higher for men than women. In 1976 white, male householders maintained a $4,500 average earnings advantage over
black males and an $8,000 average earnings advantage over
white and black female householders.

The 1960–1976 period was, then, one in which income
sources, labor force activity, and need levels within households
underwent many alterations. Certain racial gaps narrowed, others widened, but none, except perhaps female earnings differentials, closed completely. Finally, it was a period in which
the so-called typical husband–wife family household came to
characterize the living arrangements of a smaller segment of
both the white and black populations.

Studies of racial inequality that have focused on individual
earners have generally shown improvements in the position of
blacks vis-à-vis whites throughout the sixties and seventies,
whereas studies focusing on family income have shown deterioration in the relative position of blacks in the seventies. It is not
surprising that there have been conflicting assessments, for not
many of the components determining economic well-being have
remained constant for either race.

In Chapter 2, I introduced two measures of economic well-
being: per capita income of individual household members and
a household welfare ratio. Each measure incorporates an adjust-

ment for differences in household size or needs. I now want to use these measures to summarize racial differences in well-being for the 1960–1976 time period. In doing so, I will also compare welfare changes to changes in household income—an indicator that does not adjust for racial differences, or change over time, in household size or needs.

Racial Differences in Household Well-Being

In Table 6.1 average welfare ratios (i.e., income/needs), per capita income, and total income for households are presented for the three points in time I have used throughout this study: 1960, 1970, and 1976. (I have used the Consumer Price Index to convert all dollar estimates in this table and all subsequent tables to 1975 dollars.) Estimates for all black and white households and for households headed by married couples, females, and males are presented. Ratios of black to white indicators of well-being are presented along with the average annual percentage change in each indicator for the 1960–1970 and 1970–1976 time periods.

Percentage improvements in well-being were generally higher for black households throughout the 1960–1976 period than for white households, but this was partially due to the low levels at which blacks started the period. That is, the same absolute improvement in black households represented proportionally greater improvement than for white households. Despite improvements, average per capita income and household welfare ratios of blacks in 1976 were still not equivalent to levels of well-being in white households in 1960!

Between 1960 and 1970 rates of improvement were largest for husband–wife households. In the 1970s improvement was most substantial for male-headed households. Throughout the

1960–1976 period percentage improvements in well-being were lowest in the most economically disadvantaged household type, female-headed households. Because female-headed households had low levels of well-being vis-à-vis other household types in 1960, much smaller absolute improvements between 1960 and 1976 would have yielded higher percentage improvements in these households than for either husband–wife or male-headed households. The fact that percentage improvements were lowest in female-headed households indicates that differentials in well-being between female-headed and other types of households widened during the period. This fact is noteworthy, given that a growing proportion of black and white children lived and continue to live in these households and given that racial differentials in the proportions in female-headed families increased over time.

Two other interesting facts emerge from a comparison of the different measures of well-being, one having to do with racial comparisons and the other with the trend over time for each racial group.

The Understatement of Racial Inequality / Ratios of black to white household income were somewhat higher at each point than ratios of black to white household welfare ratios and higher still than ratios of black to white per capita income. The most striking difference is in the ratios for female-headed households. Average household income in black, female-headed households was about 79 percent that of white, female-headed households in 1976, whereas average per capita income was only 48 percent that of whites. Black, female-headed households have one more person on average than do white, female-headed households. That additional person is most often a dependent child. Because racial differences in household size are not trivial, use of household or family income to assess racial

Table 6.1. Racial Comparisons and Time Trends in Average Per Capita Income, Household Welfare Ratios, and Household Income

	All households					Husband–wife				
				Average annual percentage change					Average annual percentage change	
	1960	1970	1976	1960–1970	1970–1976	1960	1970	1976	1960–1970	1970–1976
Average per capita income[a]										
White	$3,466	$4,832	$5,041	+3.9%	+0.7%	$3,413	$4,792	$5,002	+4.0%	+0.7%
Black	1,699	2,613	2,911	+5.4	+1.9	1,693	2,789	3,210	+6.4	+2.5
Dollar gap (W–B)	1,767	2,219	2,130			1,720	2,003	1,792		
Ratio (B/W)	.49	.54	.58			.50	.58	.64		
Average welfare ratio										
White	1.98	2.64	2.63	+3.3	–0.1	2.11	2.88	2.90	+3.6	+0.1
Black	1.09	1.59	1.67	+4.6	+0.8	1.19	1.88	2.06	+5.8	+1.6
Ratio (B/W)	.55	.60	.63			.56	.65	.71		
Average household income[a]										
White	11,222	14,732	14,343	+3.1	–0.4	12,566	17,170	17,110	+3.7	–0.1
Black	6,525	9,260	9,222	+4.2	–0.1	7,666	12,070	12,796	+5.7	+1.0
Dollar gap (W–B)	4,697	5,472	5,121			4,900	5,100	4,314		
Ratio (B/W)	.58	.63	.64			.61	.70	.75		

	Female head			Average annual percentage change		Male head			Average annual percentage change	
	1960	1970	1976	1960–1970	1970–1976	1960	1970	1976	1960–1970	1970–1976
Average per capita income[a]										
White	$3,266	$4,288	$4,197	+3.1%	−0.4%	$5,102	$6,782	$7,777	+3.3%	+2.4%
Black	1,422	1,875	2,031	+3.2	+1.4	2,864	4,089	4,978	+4.3	+3.6
Dollar gap (W−B)	1,844	2,413	2,166			2,238	2,693	2,799		
Ratio (B/W)	.44	.44	.48			.56	.60	.64		
Average welfare ratio										
White	1.39	1.79	1.74	+2.9	−0.5	2.00	2.66	2.82	+3.3	+1.0
Black	.80	1.07	1.16	+3.4	+1.4	1.26	1.76	1.91	+4.0	+1.4
Ratio (B/W)	.58	.60	.67			.63	.66	.68		
Average household income										
White	6,266	7,851	7,414	2.5	−0.9	8,582	11,145	11,499	+3.0	+0.5
Black	4,382	5,676	5,835	2.9	+0.5	5,636	7,695	7,930	+3.7	+0.5
Dollar gap (W−B)	1,884	2,175	1,579			2,946	3,450	3,569		
Ratio (B/W)	.70	.72	.79			.66	.69	.69		

[a]Expressed in 1975 dollars.

inequality, that is, use of an indicator that makes no adjustment for racial differences in household size, understates the extent of racial inequality in economic well-being.

The Understatement of Improvements over Time / The estimate of improvement in well-being for whites and blacks is highest when per capita income is taken as the indicator, intermediate when welfare ratios are considered, and lowest when household income is used to assess trends over time. Of particular interest is the 1970–1976 change, since economic improvements made in the 1960s may have been lost in the inflationary 1970s. The trend in average household income suggests that the 1970s have been a time of deterioration in economic well-being. However, measures which take into account the fact that the average household size has decreased, particularly the per capita income measure, suggest continued improvement in the 1970s for all households except white female-headed households. While percentage improvements in household income parallel improvements in indicators which adjust for changes over time in household need levels, average improvements in household income tend to understate real improvements in the well-being of both black and white household members.

Households with Children

As can be seen from Table 6.1, at all points in time and for both races well-being in female-headed households was considerably lower than in other types of households. As noted in Chapter 3, an increasing number of children, especially black children, reside in female-headed households. Table 6.2 focuses on households with children and presents changes in the well-being of husband–wife households as contrasted with changes in female-headed households. Even though per capita income and household welfare ratios have increased in female-headed households, improvements have not kept pace with improvements in husband–wife households. Marital and living arrangement decisions of parents appear to be resulting in a widening of relative economic advantages and disadvantages of children who reside in different type households. If residing in female-headed households were a very short term arrangement, these differences might not be so important. However, for increasing numbers of children, particularly black children, living with a mother alone quite often becomes a fairly long-term arrangement. Bumpass and Rindfuss (1979:62) estimate that a third of all white children experiencing a marital disruption remain in a one-parent family for at least five years and a sixth are still in this status after 10 years. For black children who experience a divorce or separation on the part of their parents, four out of five spend at least five years without their mother remarrying and about half remain in a single parent family for the remainder of their childhood.

Measures of Well-Being and the Incidence of Poverty

Table 6.3 presents the proportion of white and black households at each time point that had welfare ratios less than one, that is, need levels greater than household income, or had per capita income levels of $2,500 or less. Either of these indicators might be taken as a measure of the proportion of households in poverty. Both indicators suggest that there is great variation across household type in the probability of poverty and both indicators show substantial racial differences at each point.

One should note that within each type of household, the proportion in poverty decreased between 1960 and 1976. Since the income measure does not incorporate public in-kind transfers and there is evidence that these benefits have been increas-

Table 6.2. Comparisons of Well-Being in Husband–Wife Households and Female-Headed Households with Children, by Race and Year

Households with children	1960	1970	1976
	Average per capita income[a]		
Whites			
Husband–wife head	$2,819	$3,896	$4,073
Female head	1,784	2,388	2,394
Ratio (female/husband–wife)	.63	.61	.59
Blacks			
Husband–wife head	1,391	2,334	2,736
Female head	953	1,378	1,483
Ratio (female/husband–wife)	.55	.54	.53
	Average welfare ratio		
Whites			
Husband–wife head	1.94	2.63	2.67
Female head	1.07	1.43	1.41
Ratio (female/husband–wife)	.69	.59	.54
Blacks			
Husband–wife	1.08	1.74	1.95
Female head	.53	.58	1.00
Ratio (female/husband–wife)	.61	.53	.51
	Percentage white children residing in		
Husband–wife households	93%	89%	87%
Female-headed households	7	9	12
	Percentage black children residing in		
Husband–wife households	75%	63%	54%
Female-headed households	22	33	44

[a]Expressed in 1975 dollars.

	Avg. annual percentage Δ 1960–1970	Avg. annual percentage Δ 1970–1976
Whites		
Husband–wife head	+3.8%	+0.8%
Female head	+3.4	0.0
Ratio (female/husband–wife)		
Blacks		
Husband–wife head	+6.8	+2.9
Female head	+4.5	+1.3
Ratio (female/husband–wife)		
Whites		
Husband–wife head	+3.6%	+0.3%
Female head	+3.4	−0.2
Ratio (female/husband–wife)		
Blacks		
Husband–wife	+6.1	+2.0
Female head	+4.5	+1.3
Ratio (female/husband–wife)		

Table 6.3. Proportion of Households in Poverty by Race, Household Type, and Year^a

	Whites			Blacks			Racial differences in percentage in poverty (W–B)		
	1960	1970	1976	1960	1970	1976	1960	1970	1976
	Proportion of households with welfare ratios < 1.00								
Total households	25.0%	18.5%	16.7%	55.4%	41.5%	40.2%	−30.4%	−23.0%	−23.5%
Husband–wife—total	19.1	11.1	9.6	49.5	27.7	22.7	−30.4	−16.6	−13.1
Children	17.4	8.9	9.1	53.9	28.7	23.6	−36.5	−19.8	−14.5
No children	21.6	13.8	10.2	41.0	25.8	21.1	−19.4	−12.0	−10.9
Female head—total	47.9	41.2	36.5	71.1	62.5	61.0	−23.2	−21.3	−24.5
Living alone	55.3	48.4	41.4	75.3	68.0	63.6	−20.0	−19.6	−22.2
Children	54.4	41.9	42.0	77.5	65.7	66.3	−23.1	−23.8	−24.3
Other	27.9	20.3	12.7	52.3	41.2	33.3	−24.4	−20.9	−20.6
Male head—total	34.7	26.4	18.8	48.4	40.4	35.4	−13.7	−14.0	−16.6
Living alone	40.1	32.1	23.3	51.0	41.7	41.2	−10.9	−9.6	−17.9
Other	26.3	16.1	9.3	44.8	38.5	23.8	−18.5	−22.4	−14.5

	Whites			Blacks			Racial differences in percentage in poverty (W–B)		
	1960	1970	1976	1960	1970	1976	1960	1970	1976
	Proportion of households in which per capita income is $2,500 or less								
Total households	38.7	25.0	20.4	69.6	53.1	47.1	−30.9	−28.1	−26.7
Husband–wife—total	37.3	21.3	18.3	69.9	46.4	38.2	−32.6	−25.1	−19.9
Children	45.5	25.7	23.7	81.2	55.3	46.2	−35.7	−29.6	−22.5
No children	24.6	15.6	12.1	48.0	29.9	24.6	−23.4	−14.3	−12.5
Female—total	48.1	38.8	29.7	77.3	68.4	63.0	−29.0	−29.6	−33.3
Living alone	46.9	37.5	23.0	70.2	58.3	45.5	−23.3	−20.8	−22.5
Children	70.6	57.4	57.6	91.0	81.2	79.8	−20.4	−23.8	−22.2
Other	32.2	23.2	15.6	59.1	47.1	37.5	−26.9	−23.9	−21.9
Male—total	32.4	23.4	13.7	48.6	39.7	30.4	−16.2	−16.3	−16.7
Living alone	32.4	23.6	13.6	42.4	33.9	28.7	−10.0	−10.3	−15.1
Other	32.5	23.1	13.9	57.0	48.9	33.6	−24.5	−25.8	−19.7

*a*Expressed in percentages.

ing and have been having some redistributive effect at the low end of the income spectrum (see Smeeding, 1977; Smolensky et al., 1977:151), these findings seem accurate. That is, the proportion in poverty declined in the 1960s and is continuing to decline for both races in the 1970s. However, there was one very significant exception to this generalization: in the 1970s, there was no decline in the incidence of poverty in female-headed households with children.[1]

The Growing Importance of Racial Differences in Household Type

Differences in well-being vary greatly by household type, with female-headed households enjoying levels of well-being considerably below those of other households. Improvements have been least substantial in female-headed households, with the result that inequality among different types of households has increased. Racial differentials in the distribution of households and persons across husband–wife, male- and female-headed households also widened between 1960 and 1976.

The racial gap in average well-being for all households results both from racial differences in levels of well-being within similar type households and from racial differences in the distribution of households and persons across husband–wife, male- and female-headed households. It proves interesting to apportion the racial gap in the per capita income of individual household members and the gap in the welfare ratios of households into two components: a household type or household living arrangement component and a "pure" well-being component. That is, suppose whites and blacks had been distributed similarly across households in 1960, 1970, and 1976, but per capita income levels by race and household type remained fixed. How much of the racial gap in well-being might have been closed? On the other hand, how much could be attributed only to differences in levels of well-being within the same type of household? Table 6.4 presents a decomposition of racial differences in per capita income and household welfare ratios into a household type component and a well-being component. Kitagawa's (1955) technique for apportioning a difference into two components is employed. For the per capita decomposition, the distribution of persons across husband–wife, female- and male-headed households is used. For household welfare ratios, the distribution of households is used. Rather than choose either the black or the white distributions and means as the standard, an average of the two is used.[2]

It is clear that the dominant factor, regardless of the indicator of well-being and the weighting scheme, is that at each point in time, levels of well-being in black households were much lower than in comparable white households. It is noteworthy, however, that racial differences in household living arrangements have increased in importance over the period. That is, in 1960 virtually none of the racial difference in per capita income and only 7 percent of the difference in welfare ratios could be attributed to the fact that blacks were more highly clustered than whites in households with the lowest level of economic well-being—households with a female head. But the proportionally greater shift among blacks than whites into female-headed households, combined with the failure of female-headed households to keep up with improvements in other type households, resulted in a significant increase in the proportion of the well-being gap attributable to living arrangement differences between blacks and whites. By 1976, 8 percent of the per capita income gap and 20 percent of the racial difference in household welfare ratios could be attributed to racial differences in distributions across husband–wife, male-, and female-headed households.

Given the actual 1960–1976 increases in per capita income

Table 6.4. Decomposition of Racial Differentials in Economic Well-Being into House-hold Type and "Pure" Well-Being Components

Components of racial differential	Per capita income[a]			Household welfare ratio		
	1960	1970	1976	1960	1970	1976
Mean						
Whites	$3,466	$4,832	$5,041	1.98	2.64	2.63
Blacks	1,699	2,613	2,911	1.09	1.59	1.67
Racial differential (W–B)	1,767	2,219	2,130	.89	1.05	.96
Total racial differential	100%	100%	100%	100%	100%	100%
Due to differences in household type distributions	0	4	8	7	14	20
Due to differences in well-being within household type	100	96	92	93	86	80

[a] Expressed in 1975 dollars.

in black and white husband–wife, male-, and female-headed households, if distributions of persons across type of household had remained as they were in 1960, average per capita income in black households might have been 5 percent or $145 higher in 1976. (In white households, the large increase in per capita income in male-headed households and the small but significant increases in proportions living in these households offset the increases in low per capita income female-headed households.) Improvements in household welfare ratios might have been 3 percent higher in white and 7 percent higher in black households if there had been no shift in the distribution of households.

Throughout the 1960–1976 period, then, the vast majority of the racial difference was due to differential levels of well-being within husband–wife, male-, and female-headed households. But because improvements were not uniform among households and because racial differences in distributions of persons and households became more dissimilar over the period, household type differences were more important to the explanation of overall black–white gaps in well-being in 1976 than in 1960.

Household Size and Income: Components of Per Capita Differentials within Household Types

Within similar type households, the average racial gap in an indicator of economic well-being, such as per capita income, is a function of two components: the racial difference in household size and the racial difference in the income flow into households. Blacks are less well-off than whites both because more persons share income and because there is less income to share on average. Per capita income may overstate the economic well-being of persons in small households, and a strict per capita assessment does not include any of the social benefits indi-

Table 6.5. Decomposition of Racial Differences in Average Per Capita Income into Household Size and Income Components and Average Household Income into Earnings and Other Income Components

Components of racial differences in average per capita and household income	Husband–wife head		Female head		Male head	
	1960	1976	1960	1976	1960	1976
Racial difference in average per capita income (W–B)[a]						
Total difference[b]	$1,720 100%	$1,792 100%	$1,844 100%	$2,166 100%	$2,238 100%	$2,799 100%
Due to household size differentials	28	27	35	46	18	12
Due to income differentials	72	73	65	54	82	88
Racial difference in average household income (W–B)[a]						
Total difference[b]	$4,895 100%	$4,314 100%	$1,884 100%	$1,579 100%	$2,946 100%	$3,569 100%
Due to difference in income other than earnings	11	19	42	57	24	21
Due to differences in earnings	89	81	58	43	76	79
from husbands/male heads	(84)	(94)	—	—	(65)	(70)
from wives/female heads	(4)	(−12)	(54)	(35)	—	—
from other household members	(1)	(−1)	(4)	(8)	(11)	(9)

[a]Expressed in 1975 dollars.
[b]Expressed in percentages.

viduals may derive from living with other persons. But per capita differentials do provide some indication of relative potentials for consumption.

Table 6.5 affords an assessment of the relative importance of income and household size. That is, racial differences in per capita income within husband–wife, female-, and male-headed households are decomposed, again using Kitagawa's (1955) technique, into two components: racial differences in distribution across household size categories (the size component) and average per capita income differences within categories of household size (the income component).[3]

The racial difference in income was the more significant factor in each type of household, both in 1960 and 1976. However, the household size component was by no means trivial, accounting for about a quarter of the gap in husband–wife households at both points, and, in female-headed households, a third of the gap in 1960, and close to half in 1976. The size component was least substantial in the small number of households with a male head, but even in these households, a sixth of the racial gap in 1960 and an eighth in 1976 was attributable to the household size component.

In the lower panel of Table 6.5, average household income differences are disaggregated into average racial differentials in earnings and other income sources. In husband–wife households, the difference in the average earnings of black and white husbands was the overriding source of overall income differentials. In male-headed households, differences in the average earnings of black and white heads were also quite important.

The income situation in female-headed households was unique in several ways. First, the racial difference in average household income was not nearly as large as in other households. Second, whereas earnings differentials were dominant in households with a husband or male head, the racial difference in average income from sources other than earnings was more

Table 6.6. Decomposition of 1960–1976 Improvement in Average Per Capita Income into Household Size and Income Components and Average Household Income into Earnings and Other Income Components

Components of 1960–1976 real improvement in average per capita and household income	Husband–wife head		Female head		Male head	
	White	Black	White	Black	White	Black
Average per capita improvement[a]						
Total improvement[b]	$1,589	$1,517	$931	$609	$2,675	$2,114
	100%	100%	100%	100%	100%	100%
Due to decline in household size	14	18	16	15	18	25
Due to increase in real income	86	82	84	85	82	75
Average household income improvement[a]						
Total improvement[b]	$4,544	$5,130	$1,148	$1,453	$2,917	$2,294
	100%	100%	100%	100%	100%	100%
Due to increase in income other than earnings	26	18	109	76	28	36
Due to increase (decline) in earned income	74	82	−9	24	72	64
from husbands/male heads	(50)	(46)	—	—	(76)	(70)
from wives/female heads	(23)	(34)	(40)	(68)	—	—
from others in the household	(1)	(2)	(−49)	(−44)	(−4)	(−6)

[a]Expressed in 1975 dollars.
[b]Expressed in percentages.

important in female-headed households—at least in 1976. Finally, partially because the difference in household income was smaller in female-headed households than in other households, the racial difference in household size was a larger component of the per capita differential as well.

In sum, in 1960 and in 1976 a large portion of the racial gap in per capita well-being of household members would have been covered if income flows into white and black households had been equal. But a significant portion of the racial gap in per capita well-being, particularly within female-headed households, would have remained, due to the fact that more persons shared income in black than in white households.

Summary: 1960–1976 Components of Change in Per Capita Well-Being

To summarize the components of the 1960–1976 per capita improvements of blacks and whites, gains within husband–wife, female-, and male-headed households are decomposed into those attributable to the decline in household size and those resulting from real increases in income.[4] Average household income improvements are disaggregated into those due to real increases in earnings of husbands or other male heads, wives or other female heads, and other household members and those due to increases in average amounts of income from sources other than earnings. These disaggregations are shown in Table 6.6. Using a logarithmic technique suggested by O'Connor (1977), ratios of 1976 to 1960 real earnings of husbands, wives, and other female and male heads are decomposed into employment, hours worked, and wage rate components in Table 6.7.[5]

As can be seen in Table 6.6, the most sizable improvements in per capita income—in dollar terms—were among persons re-

Table 6.7. *Decomposition of 1976/1960 Earnings Ratios of Black and White Husbands, Wives, Female and Male Heads into Percent Employed, Annual Hours, and Implied Wage Rate Components*

Components of 1960–1976 average earnings improvements	Husbands		Wives		Female heads		Male heads	
	White	Black	White	Black	White	Black	White	Black
Average earnings[a]								
1976	$11,395	$7,331	$2,454	$3,004	$3,261	$2,720	$7,762	$5,273
1960	9,126	5,012	1,402	1,220	2,801	1,789	5,561	3,658
Ratio 1976/1960	1.25	1.46	1.75	2.46	1.16	1.52	1.40	1.44
Total 1960–1976 improvement[b]	100%	100%	100%	100%	100%	100%	100%	100%
Due to increase/decline in percent employed	−26	−23	60	20	−9	−31	15	−25
Due to increase/decline in annual hours	−8	−1	0	22	−9	−5	9	5
Due to increase in implied wage rates (i.e., earnings/hours)	134	124	40	58	118	126	76	120

[a]Expressed in 1975 dollars.
[b]Expressed in percentages.

siding in male-headed households, and the least sizable gains were for those in female-headed households. The majority of the per capita improvement in all types of households—75 to 86 percent—occurred because of growth in real income. A much smaller but significant component was the decrease in larger households.

In husband–wife households, the majority of the household income improvement resulted from the increase in real earnings. In white households, about half came from increases in husbands' earnings and a quarter from growth in wives' earnings. Among blacks, a larger percentage of the improvement came from the increase in average earnings of wives: 34 percent of the income gain was due to wives' earnings and an additional 46 percent was attributable to average increases among black husbands. Among wives, an important part of the average earnings increase, particularly among whites, was that more wives had entered the labor force by 1976 (see Table 6.7). As I discussed in Chapter 5, wage increases occurred for women, but they were not as substantial in dollar terms as those for men.

In female-headed households, unlike husband–wife or male-headed households, increases in sources of income *other than earnings* was of most significance. The increase in the average earnings of female heads was a factor in income improvement, but in white households this increase was totally negated by the average loss in earnings from other household sources. In black households, the decline in earnings from other household members offset a large portion of the average increase in the earnings of female heads.

Between 1960 and 1976 improvements in economic well-being were substantial for both races. Gains were greater in the 1960s but continued into the 1970s in all but white female-headed households. Whether the period is heralded as one of great progress in eliminating racial inequality, however, rests on whether percentage improvements or remaining racial differentials are emphasized. That is, percentage improvements in average per capita income and household welfare ratios were greater among blacks than whites throughout the 1960s and 1970s, but the racial differences in average well-being remained extremely large in 1976. If the greater percentage improvements among blacks continue, blacks will eventually "catch up" to whites but it will not happen very quickly.

Perhaps most disquieting, as a growing share of both races, but particularly blacks, came to reside in female-headed households, inequality between female-headed and other type households increased. Sex inequality appears to have become an ever larger component of racial inequality in well-being.

Chapter 7

Issues and Implications

In the preceding chapters, I have attempted to specify the components of change in economic well-being of blacks and whites, as well as components of racial differences in well-being. The two major living arrangement shifts characterizing the 1960–1976 period were the increase in persons living alone and the growth in female-headed households with children. This study would not be complete without some discussion of the implications of those changes.

Among both races, the more dramatic change has been the increase in one-person households, yet this increase has received much less attention than the growth in one-parent families. One reason is that the growing proportion of the population residing alone is still relatively small. In 1976 only about 7 percent of all whites and blacks lived alone. Second, living alone is often a transitional arrangement. Although a small minority reside alone throughout adulthood and this group may be increasing in size, most adults marry and have children. A large part of the increase in one-person households is accounted for by young adults who will eventually marry and establish families, and by elderly women who have already completed an extensive family life cycle phase. Hence, the growth in one-person households has not usually been interpreted as a sign that family life is on the demise.

The growth in female-headed households with children, on the other hand, has been viewed as cause for alarm. The major reason for concern is that the well-being of an increasing number of children is involved. In 1976, 12 percent of white and

44 percent of black children resided in female-headed households, and these high cross-section figures underestimate the proportion of children who spend some childhood years living with only one parent, usually the mother.

The reason the growth in female-headed families with children has been such an important focus for this analysis is both because the racial differential in living arrangements of children has widened in recent years and because differences in economic well-being between husband–wife and female-headed households have also widened. Black husband–wife households appear to be making progress in attaining the same levels of well-being as whites, while black female-headed households fall ever farther behind economically.

The shifts in living arrangements of parents and their children raise the following questions: Why is there a growing differential between blacks and whites in the incidence of female family headship? What are the consequences (if any) of divorce and separation for children? Finally, what policies are needed in areas of family, work, and welfare reform to accommodate recent changes?

The Growing Racial Differential in Female Family Headship

Throughout the 1960–1976 period, two economic factors that contributed to marital disruption—a husband's unemployment and a wife's access to income other than her husband's earnings—characterized the economic situation in a higher proportion of black than white households. Given these two conditions alone, it is perhaps not surprising that female family headship has been more characteristic of blacks than whites. Black men remain more subject to unemployment and underemployment than white men, and, as my analysis demonstrated in

Chapter 5, the absolute dollar earnings gap between white and black male household heads remained extremely large in 1976. Among women, the labor force participation of black wives has typically been higher than that of whites, although differentials narrowed considerably between 1960 and 1976 as increases in employment among white wives outpaced those among blacks. Black wives have also had higher earnings relative to their husbands than has been true of white wives, due partially to the low average earnings of black males.

The puzzling question is: Why has the increase in female family headship, though significant among both races, been more accentuated among blacks? The increased similarity in black and white wives' labor force participation and earnings might lead one to suspect just the opposite result, a narrowing rather than a widening of racial differences in marital dissolution and headship. Also, racial differences in female headship are reduced considerably if blacks and whites of similar income are compared (see Gutman, 1976). Thus, a period of economic improvement in the position of blacks vis-à-vis whites, such as the 1960s and to a lesser extent the 1970s, would lead one to predict either no change or narrowing—not widening—of overall headship differences.

One answer may lie in the competing independence and income effects (discussed in Chapter 3), although such an explanation is not completely convincing. As this analysis has shown, in 1960 very low absolute levels of well-being characterized most black households. Assuming a minimum economic threshold must be reached before a woman with children can establish an independent household, the increases in welfare and women's earnings that occurred between 1960 and 1976 may have allowed a greater proportion to cross that economic threshold. That is, improvements for blacks were in the range in which independence effects were dominant. For whites, on the other hand, because average levels of well-being were considerably higher to begin with, similar economic improvements often moved white families much more firmly into the range where the income effect took precedence. Perhaps the surprising feature of the recent decades was not that the increase in black female headship was so high but that the increase among whites was as great as it was.

If an income–independence interpretation is correct, the more substantial the future economic gains of blacks, the more likely the income effect is to dominate and the more likely female headship rates are to decline. If economic factors are not of overwhelming importance in motivating marriage and living arrangement decisions, it is less clear what future trends will be. Systematic analysis and explanation of why the racial difference in female headship widened between 1960 and 1976 is a much-needed area of further research.

Consequences of Divorce and Separation for Children

As divorce rates continue to rise and the proportion of children involved increases, there is growing need to know what, if any, are the social, psychological, and economic consequences for children experiencing the disruption of their parents' marriage. Living with one parent, usually the mother, is often a transitional phase in the lives of children, but an increasing number of children experience such a transition and for many it becomes a fairly long-term arrangement.

The present analysis is quite clear in documenting the large economic differences between female-headed and husband–wife households with children. The evidence also suggests that these differentials are widening as more children come to reside with a mother only, at least for part of their childhood.

In addition to income differences between one- and two-parent families, there may be substantial differences in adult time available to children. Economists, such as Liebowitz (1974) and, more recently, Greenberg and Wolf (1980), have argued that the quantity and quality of adult time devoted to children are important determinants of later educational and earnings attainment. More effort is required to make those investments when one parent no longer resides with his or her children.

The growing divergence among racial groups in the living arrangements of children, combined with the attendant economic disparities among different household types, at the very least, raise questions about the equality of opportunity afforded the next generation of children. Few would advocate taking choice in living arrangements and childrearing away from the family, but the precarious economic situation in female-headed families does suggest that, at minimum, governmental steps aimed at insuring adequate *financial* support of children are needed in this country. The system for providing support for children in one-parent families is far less adequate in the United States than is true in many European countries, in particular Scandinavian countries and West Germany (see Finer, 1974). Currently, the major source of support for children who do not live with wage earners or who do not receive other income, such as child support from an absent parent, is Aid to Families with Dependent Children (AFDC). The system has a variety of undesirable features. Levels of support are extremely low in certain states and there is great variability in support levels by state. A strong disincentive to work is built into the system since even low earnings can reduce benefits considerably. In about half of the 50 states, two-parent families in which the principal wage earner is unemployed are ineligible to receive benefits (Levy, 1978; Sulvetta, 1978).

The issue that is raised by any welfare reform proposal is: What will be the cost to the larger society? Guaranteed income maintenance proposals for families and individuals encounter political difficulties, if the fate of the Family Assistance Plan is any indication, because there is widespread fear that such plans will create a disincentive to work (see Moynihan, 1973). On the other hand, when a welfare reform proposal has a strong employment component, such as was the case in the original Carter administration Program for Better Jobs and Income, it is rejected because the creation of public sector jobs is viewed as inefficient, the guarantee of full employment too costly.

Ideally, governmental policy would be aimed at facilitating the flow of private transfers from parents to their own children. Such a recommendation has been made by the Finer committee on single-parent families to the government of Great Britain (1974), which called for a taxed, guaranteed maintenance payment to be made to all one-parent families. The government would assume responsibility for collecting child support from the absent parent. Absent parents would be assessed according to their ability to pay, but single-parent families would receive a subsidy whether or not the absent parent could actually afford that level of support and whether or not the government was successful in collecting from the absent parent.

Although parental responsibility for children would be difficult, if not impossible, to legislate, it certainly could be encouraged by economic incentives built into the existing tax structure. MacDonald and Sawhill (1978) as well as Bane (1976) have suggested support systems for children that are variants on the notion of a guaranteed minimum maintenance payment or children's allowance. Bane has suggested that, although children's allowances are costly, one might view them as part of a lifetime insurance scheme, just as one might view divorce or separation as an insurable risk. Currently, workers are assured income in retirement years, via Social Security taxes and/or government or private pension plans. The notion might be extended to include childhood. Some earnings during one's years in the labor force might be used to "pay back" for one's early dependent years.

MacDonald and Sawhill have discussed a variant on the insurance idea in which all adults pay back into the system for the number of children they have but are also paid for rearing children.

> . . . individuals would receive a government "loan" payable in annual installments while their children were young but one that would be partially or completely repaid via higher taxes over a lifetime. It is a kind of social security in reverse. Further, it might be structured so as to redistribute income in a progressive fashion, but unlike a children's allowance, it (ideally) would not involve a redistribution of income among different-sized families. The key to implementing this scheme would be to make annual taxes and transfers for each family or individual some function of the difference between the number of minor children currently being supported and the number of children ever born to that family. One side effect would be to create incentives for people to adopt children or to act as foster or step-parents. It might also encourage greater support from absent parents in cases of divorce or separation (MacDonald and Sawhill, 1978:98–99).

If the United States moves toward more adequate, universal financial subsidy of children—whether by providing a guaranteed maintenance payment or by alterations in the existing tax-credit structure—there may be more marital disruption than currently, at least in the short run. The results of the Seattle–Denver income maintenance experiments suggest that increased dissolution will most likely be concentrated among couples least able to bear the added costs of maintaining two households. Thus, if more choice in living arrangements is afforded poor segments of society, some costs will have to be borne by the larger society. Those concerned that we have already slipped too far toward a welfare state will consider further government intervention in the family welfare area unjustified and undesirable. However, the absence of governmental assurance of minimum maintenance in effect supports the notion that children whose parents make financially unsound living arrangement decisions deserve to suffer the consequences. The absence of strong economic incentives aimed at insuring parental financial responsibility currently makes it quite easy for absent parents to discontinue support payments to their children.

The economic problems associated with living with one parent should be analyzed in greater depth, but it may well turn out to be the noneconomic, qualitative effects on children in differing living arrangements that prove more difficult to equalize. Although a host of studies exist that relate marital dissolution and father absence to delinquency, achievement in school, and psychological functioning (see Herzog and Sudia, 1973; Ross and Sawhill, 1975; Longfellow, 1979 for reviews), the evidence remains mixed, often based on small, unrepresentative samples, and weak in terms of establishing causal connections or even temporal sequences of events in children's lives. Much more information on the qualitative components of children's experience of their parents' divorce and separation and life in single-parent households is needed. Black family structure, to the extent that it differs from white family structure in extendedness and interhousehold helping behavior, may prove to be more adequate for assuring time and care to children in times of high rates of marital dissolution.

Interrelation of Employment and Family Policy

In the long run any equality of opportunity program aimed at guaranteeing race and sex equality in the workplace will have to be tied to family or living arrangement policies and vice versa. Individuals are not self-sufficient, isolated production–consumption units. Rather, individuals are tied economically as well as emotionally to other individuals—especially other individuals who are related by blood, marriage, or adoption.

Research reported in the previous chapters makes it fairly clear that there are three general areas needing considerable attention if further improvements in well-being are to reach all segments of the white and black population. These areas are male unemployment, particularly among blacks; women's employment and earnings opportunities; and the care and subsidy of children.

Male Unemployment / A fairly extensive literature exists that pinpoints some of the supposed causes of the employment and earnings difficulties of black men. Blacks are underrepresented in highly unionized industries and are concentrated in dead-end jobs in marginal industries (Beck et al., 1978; Beck, 1980). Blacks seldom receive similar amounts of on-the-job training as whites (Duncan and Hoffman, 1978) and have difficulty obtaining promotions and moving into higher-paying occupations (Stolzenberg, 1974).

Much of the research to date provides insight into how one might change black men in order to move them into more secure jobs. More difficult to assess is what changes are needed in the content and structure of existing jobs in order to insure that workers, black and white, have adequate incentives to fill them. If racial equality is to be achieved and if adequate levels of well-being are to be realized, we must focus our attention not only on how to facilitate the movement of black men into stable employment but also on how to make the nature of work itself more stable and satisfying.

Finally, there are two problems growing out of equal employment opportunity legislation such as that of the mid-1960s. One danger is that simply because laws barring discrimination in hiring and pay exist, we become complacent and assume that discrimination is a thing of the past. Further economic gains on the part of black workers may come much more slowly because they will depend on eliminating very subtle forms of discrimination within organizations. The second is that as affirmative action guidelines are set in motion, blacks will more and more frequently be subjected to the accusation or the assumption that they hold a certain position merely because of their race. We are already witnessing a period of backlash, of claims of reverse discrimination, and this may also impede blacks' economic gains in the coming decade.

Female Employment and Earnings / One interpretation of the changes in family living arrangements of the past two decades is that when the employment of women increases and when their earnings improve, they leave their husbands and imperil the economic well-being of their children as well as themselves. One solution is to encourage, or even coerce, women to return to the more traditional unpaid occupation of full-time housework and child care. But such an alternative, as Bane (1976) points out, runs counter to the long-term historical trend toward greater equality in men's and women's roles.

There is little to suggest the current high rates of marital dissolution are going to decline, although it is possible that delayed age at first marriage may increase the stability of marriages contracted in the future. Also, there will remain substantial economic advantages to couples who remain together and pool time and money resources.

Unfortunately, although women's earnings and employment opportunities have increased, they have not improved to the point that women can always adequately support themselves and their dependent children when it becomes necessary for them to do so. Women earn substantially less than men (see Chapter 5). They remain segregated in low-paying, traditionally female occupations (Oppenheimer, 1970; Blaxall and Reagan, 1976; Lloyd, 1975). They are also penalized for their discontinuous participation in the labor force, even though the discontinuity is in large part a function of their child-rearing activity.

It seems likely that the number of women who combine work in the paid labor force with child rearing will continue to increase. This analysis documents the growing significance of women's labor market roles for a majority of households' economic well-being. A strong public commitment is needed to eliminate penalties associated with movement in and out of the labor force to have and rear children. Greater availability of rewarding part-time work and more recognition of the value of investing in children—for men as well as for women—are required to facilitate the meshing of work and family roles. More equality of men's and women's roles in the workplace, if that continues to be a national goal, will not be achieved without parallel equalization of men's and women's roles within the home.

Care and Subsidy of Children / If there is one thing this study suggests, it is that much attention must be turned to insuring adequate time and money resources for children. Growing economic inequality among households raises serious questions about the equality of opportunity afforded future generations. The costs for adequately subsidizing children are substantial: Both further initiatives in employment opportunities as well as extension of current welfare coverage and alteration of tax structures may be required. In highly inflationary times, it is doubtful that improvements will be achieved very rapidly. But if the trend toward greater equality of opportunity is to continue, measures will have to be taken that, at minimum, insure greater financial security to children who live with a mother only.

As I have noted, blacks will not fully achieve equality in American society until they are as successful as whites in passing on advantages to their children. Implicit in this statement, of course, is the realization that as long as families rear children, equality of opportunity can never be achieved, merely approached. The precarious economic situation in female-headed families, combined with the growing inequality among households, suggests that as some segments of the white and black population become increasingly able to pass on advantages to their children—at least economic advantages—other segments may be falling further and further behind. Counteracting this trend in an enlightened fashion may prove to be the most challenging task of the coming decade.

Appendix

Poverty Thresholds, Family Budgets, and Household Economic Need

The SSA Official Poverty Thresholds (Orshansky)

Perhaps the most widely used estimates of the money income needs of families of various size and composition are those developed by Mollie Orshansky of the Social Security Administration (Orshansky, 1965; 1969). She originally developed two estimates: one based on the "economy" food plan and one on the slightly higher "low cost" food plan issued by the U.S. Department of Agriculture (USDA). The plans were designed to estimate the cost of a diet providing at least the minimum nutrition needed by persons of various age and sex.

Three steps were involved in arriving at poverty thresholds:

1. The Department of Agriculture plans separately estimated weekly food costs for 19 age–sex classes. Orshansky took these individual food cost figures and adjusted them for family size and composition and economies of scale. She varied the age–sex structure of members in each family size category and determined annual food budget needs. Then she weighted budget estimates by the actual distribution of families across age–sex structure categories. In this manner, she arrived at estimates

147

of average annual food budgets for families of differing size, number of children, and sex–age of head.

2. The next step was to assess additional costs of such items as housing and clothing. This was done by assuming that a family on the economy or low-cost food budgets would spend a third of its income for food. The basis for this assumption was a 1955 USDA survey of expenditures.[1] The annual food budget of a household with three or more members was multiplied by three to give a total needs figure. For households smaller than three, it was assumed that fixed costs (e.g., rent) did not decline in proportion to food costs and thus higher multipliers were used for these households—3.70 for two-person households and 4.89 for individuals.

3. Finally, figures were adjusted to take into account ur-ban–rural residence. It was argued that farmers produce some of the goods nonfarm households have to purchase and that farm families therefore do not require as much cash income to maintain adequate living standards. Originally, cash needs of farm families were valued at 60 percent of nonfarm family needs.

In 1969 two changes in this procedure were made. Poverty thresholds of farm families were raised from 60 to 85 percent of nonfarm thresholds. Additionally, it was decided that the pov-erty thresholds would be updated annually by adjusting for in-flation using the Consumer Price Index (CPI).

In the 1960s government officials, concerned about pov-erty in the United States and needing some way to measure it, adopted the Orshansky cutoffs. These cutoffs remain the official poverty standards used by the Bureau of the Census today. The Bureau of the Census currently measures family well-being and the incidence of poverty by relating total pretax, posttransfer money income of families to these poverty thresholds.

Criticisms of the SSA Measure

Major criticisms of the Orshansky cutoffs are:

1. The market basket base for the food estimates has not been changed since 1955–1956. Most certainly, consumer tastes have changed in the intervening years and these tastes have resulted in changing expenditures.

2. Regional differences in prices are in no way taken into account in the current standards; although these differences are almost certain to be crucial to determining whether or not a family is in poverty. For instance, estimates of the cost of living in various cities around the country made by the Bureau of Labor Statistics (BLS) show that, in general, it is more expensive for a low-income family to live in the West and the Northeast than it is to live in the South or the North Central region (McGraw, 1977:35, Table 3).

3. A few would argue that the multiplier of three overstates the poverty line, but most would argue that it is too low and that current thresholds understate the income level necessary to maintain a minimally adequate standard of living. The economy food budget of the Department of Agriculture, the plan upon which current thresholds are based, was meant for temporary or emergency use and is not appropriate as a long-run market basket. The poor would have to take all meals at home and have expert buying habits to attain nutritionally adequate diets on the food budgets forming the base of the current estimates.

4. Finally, it is questionable whether the CPI provides appropriate annual adjustment of the thresholds.[2]

The index (CPI) does not allow for shifting budgets, keeping expenditure weights constant despite changes in prices. Quantity weights are revised infrequently, with the last revision being over ten years old. Thus the weights are obsolete. Finally, the expenditure patterns of wage earners and clerical workers of selected urban centers represent the basis for calculating the CPI. Inasmuch as this group is not representative of the poor, it could be argued that the CPI is not a relevant measure of change in the price levels for the poor.

In sum, the use of index numbers to adjust poverty thresholds in response to price changes is of limited legitimacy (U.S. Department of Health, Education, and Welfare, 1976:22).

The BLS Family Budget Costs

A second source of family needs estimates is the lower family budget devised by the BLS. In the mid-1960s the bureau responded to a mandate "to find out what it costs a worker's family to live in the large cities of the U.S." (U.S. Department of Labor, 1969: vi). The bureau, using its 1960–1961 Consumer Expenditure Survey, arrived at cost of living estimates for a "typical" urban family of four for three income levels.[3]

The budgets were designed to estimate the "level and pattern of consumption required for the maintenance of health and social well-being, the nurturance of children, and participation in community activities." Total cost estimates (arrived at in the spring of 1967) included expenditures for food, housing, transportation, clothing, personal care, medical care, reading, and recreation. Also included were allowances for gifts, contributions, life insurance, personal income, Social Security taxes, and occupational expenses.

In 1967 the BLS devised "equivalence scales" to be used in estimating the needs of different-sized families. The assumption behind the scales is that families spending an equal proportion of income on food have attained equivalent living standards. Actual consumer expenditure surveys were used to calculate a set of numbers that could be used to adjust the income figures for the so-called typical family of four to those needed to provide an equivalent standard of living for smaller or larger families.[4]

Comparison of SSA and BLS Estimates

The BLS lower budget for a family of four in 1975 was $9,588. The SSA official poverty threshold for a nonfarm male-headed family of four with two children in 1975 was $5,456.

There are several reasons for the difference.

1. As noted earlier, the official standards are generally considered to be too low. It is for this reason that the Bureau of the Census tabulates a variety of characteristics for families and individuals with incomes below 125 percent of the official poverty threshold as well as for those persons and families at or below the actual threshold. Taking 125 percent of the official standard would yield a figure of $6,820 for a nonfarm family of four in 1975.

2. The BLS estimates include income needed for taxes, whereas the official standards ostensibly represent after-tax income needed by a family of a given size and composition.[5]

3. Also, the BLS estimates include money for recreation, gifts, occupational expenses, and some meals taken away from home. Therefore, the BLS estimates are probably not as close to a subsistence level definition of family living standards as are the official thresholds.

4. Finally, BLS estimates are derived for the largest (and presumably the most expensive) urban centers in the country.

Criticisms of the BLS Estimates

Some of the criticisms of the SSA measure are equally applicable to the BLS measure. The most serious are:

1. The estimates are derived for a typical urban family of four. Underlying the equivalence scales used to estimate needs for families of different size and composition is the assumption that families who spend the same proportion of total income on food have equivalent standards of living. Such an assumption is not unlike that which forms the basis for the SSA official poverty standards (i.e., that total costs of living for a family are three times the family food budget). This aspect of the BLS estimates is somewhat arbitrary and is open to criticisms similar to those leveled at the multiplier chosen for the SSA poverty thresholds.

2. The BLS procedures are based on the BLS's Consumer Expenditure Survey conducted in 1961, so like the official poverty thresholds that make use of 1955 and 1961 studies, the bases for the estimates are dated.

3. Additionally, BLS equivalence scales only exist for households containing one or two adults and their children. There are no derived index numbers for households containing other adults. This lack is particularly critical to my analysis, which focuses upon racial differentials in family composition as one possible explanation of differences in family welfare. An important factor is the racial differential in the presence of adults other than the household head.

Additional Considerations

Costs of Children (Espenshade and Oppenheimer) / Neither BLS estimates nor SSA poverty thresholds adequately take into account the differentials in direct costs of different-aged children. The age adjustments that are made are food cost adjustments based on 1955 and 1961 surveys. More complete studies of the direct cost of children exist.

Espenshade (1973) considered husband–wife families with

one, two, and three children. His intent was to determine the
total cost of raising children in the urban United States, and he
was especially interested in the marginal cost of second and
third children. His estimates incorporated an assumption similar to the BLS, that is, that families of different size which spend
similar portions of income on food are equally well-off. He derived estimates of the cost of children using the BLS's 1960–1961
Consumer Expenditure Survey, and computed average annual
costs—for three income levels—for children of first, second,
and third birth orders, and for ages 0–5, 6–11, and 12–17.

Since Espenshade's concern was with the marginal costs of
second and third children, his cost figures are not readily usable. Oppenheimer (1976) has taken Espenshade's estimates
and averaged and readjusted them in order to arrive at annual
average costs of various-aged children. One major conclusion
from Espenshade and Oppenheimer's work is that teenage children are expensive. Table A.1 shows in 1975 dollars the cost es-

Table A.1. Direct Costs of Children

Age	Cost[a]
Children, 0–5	$1,521
Children, 6–11	2,274
Children, 12–17	3,617
Adults (BLS)	3,356
Adults (SSA)	2,902
Ratio of adult[b]/child 12–17 = .87	
Ratio of adult/child 6–11 = 1.38	
Ratio of adult/child 0–5 = 2.06	

SOURCES: Monthly Labor Review, July 1976, p. 40; Current Population Report, P–60, No. 106, p. 198; Oppenheimer (1976):
Appendix.
[a]Expressed in 1975 dollars.
[b]SSA and BLS estimates for adults were averaged to arrive at the
cost of an adult used in these ratios.

timates for children of various ages. Also included are the SSA poverty figures and BLS low-budget figures for single adults. The ratio of costs for adults to children is the following: Adult costs are about twice those of children age 0–5; 1.4 times those of children age 6–11; and only 87 percent those of children age 12–17 (i.e., teenagers).

Opportunity Costs of Children and Housework / Another cost of children considered in the economic literature is the input of time children require. Along with this consideration, time is required to produce home goods (e.g., meals) and these time costs, which differ for households of varying size and composition, are usually not figured into poverty or need estimates.

Clair Vickery notes that minimal nonpoor levels of consumption require both money and hours of household production. For instance, official poverty standards are based on assumptions that all meals are prepared at home. The BLS typical family has a nonworking wife.

Although there is no explicit assumption that a household with income equal to the poverty standard must have a person working full time in the home to be nonpoor, this assumption does seem to be implicit in the derivation of official poverty standards (Vickery, 1977:30).

Most studies on costs of nonmarket work have been restricted to husband–wife families. Two techniques for assessing costs of child care and housework have usually been used: (1) estimate the wages foregone by the person, usually the wife, who engages in home activity and use this as a measure of opportunity costs or (2) value housework at some fixed rate (e.g., $2 or $5 an hour) and use such valuations in the analysis of well-being (see Morgan, 1978).

Using the second technique, Vickery (1977) has recently derived a set of estimates of the housework–child care time needs for households with one or two adults with 0 to 6 children.[6] She shows that one-adult households with children run a high risk of being time poor if the adult works full time in the labor market. That is, one adult cannot work full time plus have enough hours left over to accomplish the necessary home tasks required. Such a household must have income enough above poverty standards to purchase some of the necessary home goods and services or else that household will actually be poor— "time poor" as Vickery labels it. She argues persuasively that

to base the benefit schedule of an income-support program on an index that defines poverty in terms of money income alone is to create gross inequities across households that vary in their number of adult hours. The equity problem, important in itself, takes on added significance when it creates incentives for individuals to adjust their living arrangements and the problem becomes aggravated if the household structure appears to be in a transitional phase as in the 1970's (Vickery, 1977: 27–28).

Her point is important. However, adjustment of need measures for hours of adult labor available is not a simple or straightforward task. Vickery's own analysis is not very helpful in this regard, since it is conducted under the hypothetical condition that all adults work full time in the labor market. When the analysis is of actual households, as it is here, it becomes less clear how one should translate time needs and assets of households into dollar terms.

In 1976 the Panel Study of Income Dynamics, a longitudinal survey of over 5,000 households, obtained information from heads (and spouses) of households on the number of hours spent by all household members "cooking, cleaning and doing other work around the house" and "looking after kids and taking them places" (Morgan, 1976).

Using the 1976 panel data, I have estimated the average number of housework and child care hours needed by households with one, two, or three or more adults, and with zero, one, two, or three or more children aged 0–5, 6–13, and 14–17.

Results from the multiple classification analysis are presented in Table A.2. As one would expect, preschoolers were most costly in terms of time, followed by children 6–13 and then by teenagers and adults. In 1976, on average, households spent about 1,900 hours a year or about 37 hours a week in housework and child care.

Table A.2. Multiple Classification Analysis Predicting Annual Housework and Child Care Hours for Households in 1976

	Sample n	Gross effect	Net effect
Number of adults			
One	1,683	−1,173.9	−816.7
Two	3,284	448.2	279.0
Three or more	735	684.9	622.8
Number of children, 0–5			
None	4,556	−375.0	−1,303.2
One	833	1,379.2	1,049.6
Two	261	1,848.8	1,685.4
Three or more	52	1,493.2	1,293.9
Number of children, 6–13			
None	4,304	−347.4	−197.9
One	770	805.8	342.9
Two	444	1,239.3	756.7
Three or more	184	1,764.7	1,368.2
Number of children, 14–17			
None	4,799	−148.0	−71.7
One	595	554.6	254.3
Two	261	1,163.8	593.9
Three or more	46	1,654.7	821.3
Grand mean		1,935.2	
R^2		.490	

SOURCE: Data from the ninth wave of the Panel Study of Income Dynamics.

Table A.3. Comparison of Vickery's Estimates of Weekly Housework and Child Care Hours with Estimates Derived from the Panel Study of Income Dynamics

Household type	Estimates from panel data[a]	Vickery's estimate
One adult with		
0 children	10	31
1 child	17–36	57
2 children	23–49	61
3 children	28–59	61
Two adults with		
0 children	31	43
1 child	38–57	62
2 children	44–70	66
3 children	49–80	66
Total sample (average)	37.2	

[a]Range is given. The value differs depending upon the age of the child (children).

Table A.3 compares these results with estimates Vickery (1977) derived from 1967 time budget data from a sample of husband–wife couples in Syracuse, New York. Estimates from the panel data are reasonable, but somewhat lower than Vickery's estimates. While Vickery's time budget data may be somewhat more complete, the national sample of households from which the panel estimates are derived is more representative of all household types.

The problem with all empirical estimates of housework and child care hours is of course that estimates are of what *is* rather than what *is truly necessary*. Vanek (1974), for instance, found that housewives spent 55 hours a week on housework in the 1960s while employed women averaged 27 hours a week. This differential did not result because other household members made up the difference in families with an employed wife. Rather, housework time was to some extent expandable or contractable depending upon the time available.

Construction of the Household Need Measure Used in My Analysis

For my analysis, procedures similar to Orshansky's, but adjusted somewhat, were used in arriving at household need levels. The major differences between this procedure and Orshansky's are:

1. Differential direct costs for children of various ages are explicitly figured into any particular household's needs level. Thus, a husband and wife with two preschoolers are determined to have fewer needs than a husband and wife with two teenagers.

2. Beyond age 18 no sex and age differences in needs are allowed. All adults are considered to need the same amount of money and household size is the only variation introduced, in order to adjust for economies of scale.

In USDA food plans, food costs decrease at older ages and are less for teenage and adult women than for teenage and adult men. Following Orshansky's procedure of multiplying food costs by three to arrive at total costs, young males end up needing more than older males and females. Thus, households with female heads or aged heads are considered to have lower needs than are households with male heads. If one were concerned with just food needs, the age–sex differential would be justified. But, as Morgan (1978) has argued, sex and age differences in food needs are not usable because other need differentials may well offset them.

3. Results from the 1976 panel study data on housework

and child care are used to make adjustments for household time shortages.

For this analysis, I averaged 1967 U.S. Department of Agriculture food estimates published in March, June, and September.[7] Since 1967 is the base year for the Consumer Price Index, it seemed a desirable starting point for average food estimates. I arrived at the following schedule using the low-cost food plans (i.e., rather than the economy food plans generally considered to be too low).

Age	Average Weekly Food Cost (1967 Dollars)
4	4.0
4–6	4.6
7–9	5.5
10–12	6.4
13–15	7.3
16–20	8.0
21–35	7.0
36–55	6.7
55+	5.9

Since it seemed desirable to eliminate cost differences for age as well as sex among adults, the first step was to take, as Morgan (1978) has, the $7 figure for young adults and use this as a food standard for all adults.

If the ratios of children of various ages to adults that Oppenheimer's calculations imply are taken as valid, weekly food costs for children would be the following:

Age Ratio	Cost Ratio	Cost for Children
18+/12–17	$.87 = \$7/x$	$x \cong \$8$ for 12–17 year olds
18+/6–11	$1.36 = \$7/x$	$x \cong \$5$ for 6–11 year olds
18+/0–5	$2.06 = \$7/x$	$x \cong \$3.5$ for 0–5 year olds

These food cost estimates by children's ages seemed roughly in line with Department of Agriculture calculations except that costs for the youngest age group were a bit low. Thus a figure of $4 seemed more appropriate for 0–5 year olds.

For each household, an annual food cost in 1967 dollars was arrived at by summing individual costs. Next, an adjustment for economies of scale for larger households was introduced.[8] For single-person households, 20 percent was added; for households of two, 10 percent was added; for three, 5 percent was added; for five, 5 percent was subtracted; and for households of six or more, 10 percent was subtracted. Then these adjusted food budgets were multiplied by 3.0 for households of three or more, by a factor of 3.7 for two-person households, and 4.89 for single persons.

Household need standards were calculated in 1967 dollars. These were multiplied by 1.612 (i.e., the ratio of the CPI for 1975 to that for base year 1967) to arrive at needs levels for 1975.

A final step was to enter the adjustment for time shortages in households. Using the multiple classification results already described, I calculated a total number of hours of housework/child care for each household. That is, the number and ages of members were used to arrive at the average annual hours of housework for a household.

Every adult in the household was considered eligible to contribute housework time. In any given year an adult has 168 hours per week, or 8,760 hours per year, available. Estimates of necessary personal time (i.e., sleeping, eating, and personal care) range from 72 hours per week (Robinson, 1977) to 81 hours per week (Vickery, 1977). In my calculations, an intermediate figure of 77 hours per week, or 11 hours per day, were allowed each adult. Out of a person's 8,760 annual hours, 4,745 were available for market and nonmarket work and leisure. From this figure I subtracted the annual number of hours an adult worked (i.e., hours of market work in the week preceding the survey times weeks worked the previous year). The remaining hours represented the maximum hours each adult had available for child care and housework. This figure was summed over adults to arrive at the total number of hours a household had for non-market work. The estimate of the hours needed by the household for housework and child care was subtracted from the available hours and if the resulting number was negative (i.e., if there was a time shortage in the household), the number of hours the household was short was multiplied by $4.00 an hour. This amount was then added to the household need estimates.[9]

A Note on the Absence of a Regional Adjustment

The needs construction described contains no adjustments for regional differences in costs of living. The state in which a household is located and whether or not the household is in an SMSA is information given in the 1960 and 1970 census data. No finer distinctions are available, however. With the 1976 CPS, information is provided on whether or not households are located in one of the 35 largest SMSA's.

Using 1976 CPS data, I constructed a needs measure with a regional adjustment. BLS ratios of costs of living for low-income families in the largest SMSA's were used to make the adjustment (McGraw, 1977). BLS estimates did not exist for all the SMSA's identified on the March 1976 CPS tape so an average for all SMSA's was used for some households. In addition, for households not in an SMSA, an average figure for nonmetropolitan areas was used. This was the best regional adjustment that could be made.

Table A.4 presents the distribution of a household welfare ratio (i.e., income/needs) in which the denominator contains a regional adjustment and compares it with one which does not. Dissimilarity in the distributions across the two measures are re-

Table A.4. Dissimilarity in the Distribution of 1976 Household Welfare Ratio Distributions with and without an Adjustment for Regional Differences in the Cost of Living

Household welfare ratio	White			Black		
	Regional adjustment	No regional adjustment	Dissimilarity	Regional adjustment	No regional adjustment	Dissimilarity
<.50	3.64%	3.89%	.25%	11.39%	12.67%	1.28%
.50– .99	12.06	12.61	.55	26.42	27.28	.86
1.00–1.49	12.88	13.39	.51	16.29	15.80	–.49
1.50–1.99	12.84	13.06	.22	12.84	12.56	–.28
2.00–2.49	12.84	12.90	.06	10.15	9.88	–.27
2.50–2.99	11.59	11.65	.06	7.63	7.05	–.58
3.00–3.49	9.21	9.00	–.21	5.58	5.45	–.13
3.50–3.99	6.93	6.52	–.41	3.39	3.26	–.13
4.00 and over	18.01	16.97	–1.04	6.31	6.06	–.25
	100.0%	100.0%	1.66%	100.0%	100.0%	2.14%

ported for all black and white households. The distributions are quite close (i.e., there was only about a 2 percent difference for either black or white households). The regional adjustment leads to a slightly lower estimate of the proportion in poverty than does the measure without the adjustment. Although a regional adjustment is theoretically defensible, because the same adjustment could not be made for all time points and because even the most refined adjustment that could be made was still too crude to make much difference in welfare ratio distributions, no regional adjustment was included in the measure used in this analysis.

Notes

Chapter 1
1. Plotnick and Skidmore, in discussing poverty in the 1965–1972 period, note the following:

> During this period, the fastest growth in living units was among unrelated individuals and families with female heads. Increasing numbers of young and elderly persons and women with children have established independent households in recent years. Because these groups are more likely to be pretransfer poor than are families with prime-age male heads, this change has increased the overall incidence of pretransfer poverty. This trend toward living apart from relatives has been encouraged by changing attitudes toward divorce, marriage, and nuclear and extended family, and by rising incomes, including transfers, which enable persons to live independently by ensuring their financial security. If these shifts in the living arrangements of Americans had not occurred between 1965 and 1972, we estimate that absolute pretransfer poverty would have affected about 23.7 percent of all households in 1972 (instead of 24.8 percent) and the income gap would have been about $2 billion lower (1975:138).

Income gap refers to the amount of money required to bring all persons up to official poverty thresholds.

Chapter 2
1. One difference in procedures between the census and the CPS that does have some effect on this analysis is that the living arrangements of college students are handled differently. Students away at college are not considered household members in the 1970 census but are enumerated as household members in the 1976 CPS. This noncom-

parability is unfortunate and should be kept in mind. Since my focus is not specifically on the living arrangements of young adults, however, this difference probably does not affect results presented here to a great extent.

2. Beginning in 1978 the U.S. Bureau of the Census discontinued use of the term "head." The person, or one of the persons, in whose name a unit is owned or rented, is designated as the reference person and the relation of all other persons to this reference person is determined. In this analysis, the term head is used because data were collected using this concept and because the term is commonly used and understood in both the professional literature and the popular press.

3. The 1976 figures are weighted to correct for the different probabilities of selection into the sample. The March supplement weight for the household head is used (see U.S. Bureau of the Census, 1977:8).

4. Estimates appear annually in the P–60 series of the *Current Population Reports* issued by the U.S. Bureau of the Census.

5. BLS procedures, for example, make it difficult to arrive at costs in multiple adult households because equivalence scales are derived for families of one or two adults and varying numbers of children.

6. These economy-of-scale adjustments were those used by Orshansky and have also been employed by Morgan (1976:109) in work with the Panel Study of Income Dynamics.

Chapter 3

1. There have been small fluctuations in the proportion of children living with their father only and at all dates, about 1 percent of the white and 2 percent of the black children were in this status. Since 1960 there has been a modest decline in the proportion who live with neither parent, but the racial difference in this indicator remains very large. About 9 percent of the black contrasted to 2 percent of the white children lived with neither their father nor their mother in 1976 (U.S. Bureau of the Census, 1977b: Table 5).

Chapter 4

1. The 1976 CPS actually asked a question on usual hours of employment in the weeks a person worked the previous year. An alternate measure of annual hours was constructed for 1976 using this weekly hours variable. The two annual hours constructions were similar, although the variable using "usual hours worked last year" gave slightly higher mean estimates of annual hours worked. To maintain com-

parability between 1960 and 1976, hours past week times weeks past year is used in the analysis of both time points.

2. In 1960, 40.3 percent of white female-headed households with children had other adults present and 75.9 percent of these households received earnings from those other adults. Thus in 30 percent of white households (i.e., 40.3% × 75.9%), earnings from others were present. Similarly, in 40 percent of black female-headed households with children (i.e., 50.2% × 77.4%), there were earnings contributions from other adults.

Chapter 5

1. An important exception is that among black prime-working-age males (i.e., those 25 to 49 years of age), proportions working full time actually increased between 1960 and 1976.

2. Technically, a dependent variable that is a dichotomy is inappropriate here. Gillespie (1977:117) reports, however, that when the split on the dependent variable for a sample as a whole is around 50/50, violation of statistical assumptions is often inconsequential.

3. The Duncan Socioeconomic Index (SEI) is a widely used procedure for assigning an ordered prestige score to occupations. The derivation is described in detail in O. D. Duncan (1961). The SEI scores are obtained by regressing survey respondents' prestige ratings of an occupation on the education and income characteristics of workers in that occupation. Duncan's work was based on a 1947 survey of the U.S. population and 1950 census data. Featherman and Hauser (1975) have updated that work for occupational categories used in the 1970 census.

4. These regressions were also run using a log transformation of earnings as the dependent measure. Results were essentially the same. Dollar earnings regressions were presented because the coefficients are intuitively easier to understand.

Chapter 6

1. The absence of a decline in poverty among female-headed families with children explains, in part, why there has been an actual increase in the absolute number of black persons in poverty in the 1970s (see U.S. Bureau of the Census, 1979:Table C). An increasing share of the poverty population is comprised of women and their dependent children.

2. Decomposition follows Kitagawa (1955, 1964) and was accomplished according to the following formula:

$$(\overline{W}_w - \overline{W}_b) \quad = \quad \sum_{i=1}^{n} ((p_{iw} - p_{ib}) \cdot \overline{W}_{ib}) \quad +$$

Mean Racial $\quad=\quad$ Difference in Household Type
Difference in a $\qquad\qquad$ Distributions
Measure of Well-
Being

$$\sum_{i=1}^{n} ((\overline{W}_{iw} - \overline{W}_{ib}) \cdot p_{ib}) \quad +$$

Differences in Well-Being
Within Household Type
Categories

$$\sum_{i=1}^{n} (W_{iw} - W_{ib}) (p_{iw} - p_{ib})$$

Interaction

The decomposition was accomplished using blacks as weights, as is shown in the equation. Alternately, the decomposition was done using whites as weights. The interaction component was small and accounted for less than 6 percent of the total racial difference. If whites were used as weights, the household type component would be somewhat smaller than that reported in Table 6.4. If blacks were used as weights, the household type component would be somewhat larger than that reported in the table. In that table neither whites or blacks were chosen as the standard. Rather, an average of the two weighting schemes was used, and the interaction was subsumed in each of the two components.

3. The procedure for the per capita decomposition is analogous to that described in note 2 and follows Kitagawa (1955, 1964). The interaction ranged from 6 percent in the 1976 decomposition for husband–wife households to 19 percent in the 1960 decomposition in female-headed households. That is, the interaction component was more sizable than in the decomposition reported in Table 6.4 and the apportionment of per capita differentials into separate size and income components is approximate.

The household income disaggregation is accomplished according to the formula

$$(\bar{I}_w - \bar{I}_b) \quad = \quad (\bar{O}_w - \bar{O}_b) \quad + \quad (\bar{E}_w - \bar{E}_b)$$

Mean Total Household $\quad=\quad$ Mean Differences in $\quad+\quad$ Mean Differences in
Income Difference $\qquad$ Income from Sources $\qquad$ Income from Earnings
$\qquad\qquad$ Other than Earnings

$$(\bar{E}_w - \bar{E}_b) = (\bar{H}_w - \bar{H}_b) + (\bar{W}_w - \bar{W}_b) + (\bar{OTT}_w - \bar{OTH}_b)$$

| Mean Total Household Earnings Differences | = | Mean Differences in Husbands/ Male Heads' Earnings | + | Mean Differences in Wives/Female Heads' Earnings | + | Mean Differences in Earnings from Other Household Members |

4. The procedure for the per capita decomposition is analogous to that described in note 2. As with the decomposition reported in Table 6.4, interactions were small and ranged from 3 percent for the decomposition in white husband–wife households to 8 percent for the decomposition in black husband–wife households.

The procedure for the household income disaggregation is analogous to that described in note 3.

5. Following the suggestion of O'Connor (1977), a logarithmic technique is used to decompose 1976 to 1960 earnings ratios into an employment component, an annual hours component, and a wage rate component. That is,

$$E_i = LFP_i \cdot HRS_i \cdot WAGE_i,$$

where i is either husbands, wives, other male or female heads in 1960 or 1976,

E is average annual earnings of group i,

LFP is the percentage with earnings (the percentage employed) in the previous year,

HRS is the average annual hours worked by employed persons, and WAGE is the average earnings per hour of employed persons.

Taking the natural logarithm of the 1976 to 1960 ratios allows for a simple interpretable apportionment of the earnings improvement to that attributable to changes in percentage employed, annual hours worked, and wage rates. That is,

$$\ln(E_{i76}) - \ln(E_{i60}) = \ln(LFP_{i76}) - \ln(LFP_{i60}) +$$
Total Earnings Differential   Differential in percentage employed
$$\ln(HRS_{i76}) - \ln(HRS_{i60}) +$$
Differential in annual hours worked
$$\ln(WAGE_{i76}) - \ln(WAGE_{i60})$$
Differential in (implied) wage rates.

Appendix

1. Orshansky (1965:33) actually determined that a multiplier of three was appropriate *if* the low-cost food plan figures were used, but that a multiplier of four was probably more appropriate if economy food plan figures were used. Eventually, the economy food figures—with a multiplier of three, not four—were adopted by the government as official standards.

Zimbalist (1977) claims that better figures available from a 1961 Bureau of Labor Statistics survey would indicate that a multiplier of 3.4 should have been used—about a 13.3 percent increase. He asserts that the low-cost figures and a multiplier of 3.4 were not used for political reasons. Such figures would have shown one-third of the families in the United States in poverty and this was politically unacceptable. Preconceived notions were that one-fifth were in poverty. The economy plan and a multiplier of three fit that notion.

2. The BLS has actually revised the CPI in 1978 and this revised index will be used to inflate thresholds in the future.

3. The typical family of four consisted of a male family head, age 38, working full time, his nonworking wife, and their 13-year-old son and 8-year-old daughter.

4. Adjustment procedures are described in detail in "Revised Equivalence Scale for Estimating Incomes or Budget Costs by Family Type," U.S. Bureau of Labor Statistics, Bulletin No. 1570–2, 1968.

5. This is usually ignored, however, as for example when the Bureau of the Census divides total pretax income of a family by the poverty threshold to determine which families are in or out of poverty. No adjustment for taxes is made.

6. Vickery makes use of time budget data collected from 1,400 husband–wife households in a 1967 study done in Syracuse, New York.

7. *Family Economics Review*, 1967.

8. The procedure is adopted from the Panel Study of Income Dynamics. It is the same procedure that Orshansky used in arriving at official poverty thresholds (personal communication with James Morgan).

9. In 1976, the average hourly wage of persons working in service industries was about $4 (U.S. Department of Labor, 1975:99).

Bibliography

Allison, Paul
    1978   "Measures of Inequality." American Sociological Review 45 (December): 865.

Althauser, Robert P. and Michael Wigler
    1972   "Standardization and component analysis." Sociological Methods and Research 1 (August): 97–135.

Bane, M. J.
    1976   Here to Stay: American Families in the Twentieth Century. New York: Basic Books.

Beck, E. M.
    1980   "Labor unionism and racial income inequality." American Journal of Sociology 85 (January): 791–814.

Beck, E. M., P. M. Horan, and C. M. Tolbert II
    1978   "Labor market segmentation and discrimination against minorities." Paper presented at the annual meeting of the American Sociological Association, San Francisco (September).

Becker, Gary S.
    1967   Human Capital and the Personal Distribution of Income: An Analytical Approach. Ann Arbor: University of Michigan Press.

Bergmann, B.
    1971   "The effect on white incomes of discrimination in employment." Journal of Political Economy 79 (March/April): 294–313.

Bianchi, S. M.
    1980   "Racial differences in per capita income, 1960–76: the importance of household size, headship, and labor force participation." Demography 17 (May): 129–144.

Bianchi, S. M. and R. Farley
    1979   "Racial differences in family living arrangements and economic well-being: an analysis of recent trends." Journal of Marriage and the Family 41 (August): 537–551.

Billingsley, Andrew
  1968   Black Families in White America. Englewood Cliffs: Prentice-
          Hall.
Blau, Francine
  1975   "Longitudinal patterns of female labor force participation." In
          Dual Careers: A Longitudinal Analysis of the Labor Market
          Experience of Women. Vol. 4. Columbus: Center for Human
          Resources, Ohio State University.
Blau, Peter M. and O. D. Duncan
  1967   The American Occupational Structure. New York: John Wiley
          and Sons.
Blaxall, M. and B. Reagan (eds.)
  1976   Women and the Workplace: The Implications of Occupational
          Segregation. Chicago: University of Chicago Press.
Bowen, W. C. and T. A. Finegan
  1969   The Economics of Labor Force Participation. Princeton:
          Princeton University Press.
Bradbury, K.
  1978   "Income maintenance alternatives and family composition:
          an analysis of price effects." Journal of Human Resources 13
          (Summer): 305–331.
Brown, Gary P.
  1976   "How type of employment affects earnings differences by
          sex." Monthly Labor Review 99 (July): 25–30.
Bumpass, L. and R. R. Rindfuss
  1979   "Children's experience of marital disruption." American Jour-
          nal of Sociology 85 (July): 49–65.
Bumpass, Larry L. and James A. Sweet
  1972   "Differentials in marital instability, 1970." American So-
          ciological Review 37 (December): 754–766.
Burch, T. K.
  1970   "Some demographic determinants of average household size:
          an analytical approach." Demography 7 (February): 61–69.
Burstein, P.
  1979   "EEO legislation and the income of women and nonwhites."
          American Sociological Review 44 (June): 367–391.
Cain, Glen
  1966   Married Women in the Labor Force: An Economic Analysis.
          Chicago: University of Chicago Press.

Carliner, Geoffrey
  1975 "Determinants of household headship." Journal of Marriage and the Family 37 (February): 28–39.

Carter, Hugh and Paul C. Glick
  1970 Marriage and Divorce: A Social and Economic Study. Cambridge: Harvard University Press.

Cherlin, A.
  1978 "Employment, income, and family life: the case of marital dissolution." In Women's Changing Roles at Home and on the Job. Proceedings of a Conference on the National Longitudinal Surveys of Mature Women. Special Report No. 26. Washington, D.C.: National Commission for Manpower Policy.

Chilman, Catherine S.
  1975 "Families in poverty in the early 1970s: rates, associated factors, some implications." Journal of Marriage and the Family 37 (February): 49–62.

Coe, R. D.
  1976 "Sensitivity of the incidence of poverty to different measures of income." In G. Duncan and J. Morgan (eds.), Five Thousand American Families—Patterns of Economic Progress. Vol. 5. Ann Arbor: Institute for Social Research, University of Michigan.
  1977 "Dependency and poverty in the short and long run." In G. Duncan and J. Morgan (eds.), Five Thousand American Families—Patterns of Economic Progress. Vol. 4. Ann Arbor: Institute for Social Research, University of Michigan.

Cohen, Malcolm S.
  1969 "Married women in the labor force: an analysis of participation rates." Monthly Labor Review 92 (October): 31–35.

Conte, Michael
  1976 "Labor market discrimination against women." In G. Duncan and J. Morgan (eds.), Five Thousand American Families—Patterns of Economic Progress. Vol. 4. Ann Arbor: Institute for Social Research, University of Michigan.

Cooney, Rosemary S.
  1979 "Demographic components of growth in white, black, and Puerto Rican female-headed families: comparison of the Cutright and Ross/Sawhill methodologies." Social Science Research 8 (June): 144–158.

Corcoran, Mary
    1976   "Work experience, work interruption, and wages." In G.
            Duncan and J. Morgan (eds.), Five Thousand American Fam-
            ilies—Patterns of Economic Progress. Vol. 6. Ann Arbor: In-
            stitute for Social Research, University of Michigan.
Corcoran, M. and G. J. Duncan
    1979   "Work history, labor force attachment, and earnings dif-
            ferences between races and sexes." Journal of Human Re-
            sources 14 (Winter): 3–20.
Cutright, Phillips
    1970   "Income and family events: getting married." Journal of Mar-
            riage and the Family 32 (November): 628–637.
    1971a   "Income and family events: family income, family size, and
            composition." Journal of Marriage and the Family 33 (Febru-
            ary): 161–173.
    1971b   "Income and family events: marital stability." Journal of Mar-
            riage and the Family 33 (May): 291–306.
    1972   "Illegitimacy in the U.S.: 1920–68." In C. Westoff and R.
            Parke (eds.), Commission on Population Growth and the
            American Future. Vol. 1: Demographic and Social Aspects of
            Population Growth. Washington, D.C.: U.S. Government
            Printing Office.
    1974   "Components of change in the number of female family
            heads aged 15–44: U.S., 1940–70." Journal of Marriage and
            the Family 36 (November): 714–721.
Danziger, S. and R. Plotnick
    1977   "Demographic change, government transfers, and income."
            Monthly Labor Review 100 (April): 7–11.
Davis, K.
    1972   "The American family in relation to demographic change." In
            C. Westoff and R. Parke (eds.), Commission of Population
            Growth and the American Future. Vol. 1: Demographic and
            Social Aspects of Population Growth. Washington, D.C.: U.S.
            Government Printing Office.
Dickinson, J.
    1974   "Labor supply of family members." In J. Morgan (ed.), Five
            Thousand American Families—Patterns of Economic Prog-
            ress. Vol. 1. Ann Arbor: Institute for Social Research, Univer-
            sity of Michigan.

Dickinson, Katherine
1974   "Transfer income." In J. Morgan (ed.), Five Thousand Ameri-
        can Families—Patterns of Economic Progress. Vol. 1. Ann Ar-
        bor: Institute for Social Research, University of Michigan.
1975   "Wage rates of heads and wives." In G. Duncan and J. Mor-
        gan (eds.), Five Thousand American Families—Patterns of
        Economic Progress. Vol. 3. Ann Arbor: Institute for Social Re-
        search, University of Michigan.
Dickinson, K. P. and J. C. Dickinson
1973   "Labor force participation of wives: the effects of components
        of husband's income." In Lewis Mandel et al. (eds.), Surveys
        of Consumers, 1971–72—Contribution to Behavioral Eco-
        nomics. Ann Arbor: Institute for Social Research, University
        of Michigan.
Dickinson, Peter
1973   "Race and economic inequality, 1960–67." Working Paper
        73–25. Madison: Center for Demography and Ecology, Uni-
        versity of Wisconsin.
Duncan, G.
1976   "Unmarried heads of households and marriage." In G. Dun-
        can and J. Morgan (eds.), Five Thousand American Fam-
        ilies—Patterns of Economic Progress. Vol. 4. Ann Arbor: In-
        stitute for Social Research, University of Michigan.
Duncan, Greg J. and Saul Hoffman
1978   "Training and earnings." In G. Duncan and J. Morgan (eds.),
        Five Thousand American Families—Patterns of Economic
        Progress. Vol. 6. Ann Arbor: Institute for Social Research,
        University of Michigan.
Duncan, G. and J. Morgan (eds.)
1975–   Five Thousand American Families—Patterns of Economic
1979   Progress. Vols. 3–7. Ann Arbor: Institute for Social Research,
        University of Michigan.
Duncan, O. D.
1961   "A socioeconomic index for all occupations." Pp. 109–138 in
        A. J. Reiss, Jr. (ed.), Occupations and Social Status. New
        York: Free Press.
1969   "Inheritance of poverty or inheritance of race?" In Daniel
        Moynihan (ed.), On Understanding Poverty. New York: Basic
        Books.

Duncan, O. D., David Featherman, and Beverly Duncan
1968   Socioeconomic Background and Achievement. New York: Basic Books.

Espenshade, T.
1973   The Cost of Children in Urban United States. Population Monograph Series, No. 14. Berkeley: Institute of International Studies, University of California.

Farkas, Greg
1976   "Education, wage rates, and the division of labor between husband and wife." Journal of Marriage and the Family 38 (August): 473–483.

Farley, R.
1964   "The quality of demographic data for nonwhites." Demography 1: 1–10.
1970   Growth of the Black Population. Chicago: Markham.
1977   "Trends in racial inequalities: Have the gains of the 1960s disappeared in the 1970s?" American Sociological Review 42 (April): 189–208.
1979   "Racial progress in the last two decades: What can we determine about who benefited and why?" Paper presented at the annual meeting of the American Sociological Association, Boston (August).

Farley, R. and A. Hermalin
1971   "Family stability: a comparison of trends between blacks and whites." American Sociological Review 36 (February): 1–17.
1972   "The 1960s: a decade of progress for blacks?" Demography 9 (August): 353–370.

Featherman, D. and R. Hauser
1975   "A manual for coding occupations and industries into 1970 categories and a listing of 1970-base Duncan socioeconomic and NORC prestige scores." Madison: Center for Demography and Ecology, University of Wisconsin.
1976   "Sexual inequalities and socioeconomic achievement in the U.S., 1962–73." American Sociological Review 41 (June): 462–483.
1978   Opportunity and Change. New York: Academic Press.

Ferriss, Abbott
1971   Indicators of Trends in Status of American Women. New York: Russell Sage.

Finer, M. (ed.)
1974   Report of the Committee on One-Parent Families. Command
        Paper 56290, Vols. 1 and 2. Parliamentary Papers (House of
        Commons and Command) Vol. 16. London: Her Majesty's
        Stationery Office.

Frankel, M. R.
1971   Inferences from Sample Surveys. Ann Arbor: Institute for So-
        cial Research, University of Michigan.

Fuchs, V.
1971   "Differences in hourly earnings between men and women."
        Monthly Labor Review 94 (May): 9–15.

1974   "Women's earnings: recent trends and long-run prospects."
        Monthly Labor Review 97 (May): 23–26.

Garfinkel, I. and R. H. Haveman
1974   "Earnings capacity and the target efficiency of alternative
        transfer programs." American Economic Review 64 (May):
        196–204.

Gillespie, Michael W.
1977   "Log-linear techniques and the regression analysis of dummy
        dependent variables." Sociological Methods and Research 6
        (August): 103–122.

Glick, Paul C.
1975   "A demographer looks at American families." Journal of Mar-
        riage and the Family 37 (February): 15–27.

Glick, P. C. and A. J. Norton
1971   "Frequency, duration, and probability of marriage and di-
        vorce." Journal of Marriage and the Family 33 (May): 307–
        317.

1973   "Perspectives on the recent upturn in divorce and remar-
        riage." Demography 10 (August): 301–314.

1977   "Marrying, divorcing, and living together in the U.S. today."
        Population Bulletin 32 (5). Washington, D.C.: Population Ref-
        erence Bureau.

Green, G. and E. Welniak
1980   "Measuring the effect of changing family composition on
        black–white differences in income." Paper presented at the
        annual meeting of the Population Association of America,
        Denver.

Greenberg, D. and D. Wolf
1980   "Economic consequences of experiencing parental marital

disruption." Paper presented at the annual meeting of the Population Association of America, Denver (April).

Griliches, Z. and W. Mason
1972   "Education, income, and ability." Journal of Political Economy 80 (May/June): 74–103.

Gutman, H. G.
1976   The Black Family in Slavery and Freedom, 1759–1925. New York: Pantheon.

Hampton, Robert L.
1975   "Marital disruption: some social and economic consequences." In G. Duncan and J. Morgan (eds.), Five Thousand American Families—Patterns of Economic Progress. Vol. 3. Ann Arbor: Institute for Social Research, University of Michigan.
1979   "Husband's characteristics and marital disruption in black families." Sociological Quarterly 20 (2) (Spring): 255–266.

Hannan, Michael T., N. B. Tuma, and L. P. Groeneveld
1977   "Income and marital events: evidence from an income maintenance experiment." American Journal of Sociology 82 (May): 1186–1211.
1978   "Income and independence effects on marital dissolution: results from the Seattle and Denver Income Maintenance Experiments." American Journal of Sociology 84 (November): 611–633.

Harrison, Bennett
1972   "The theory of the dual economy." Pp. 269–287 in B. Silverman and M. Yanowitch (eds.), The Worker in "Post-Industrial" Capitalism, 1974. New York: Free Press.

Haworth, J. G., J. Gwartney, and C. Haworth
1975   "Earnings, productivity, and changes in employment discrimination during the 1960s." American Economic Review 70 (March): 158–168.

Hayghe, Howard
1976   "Families and the rise of working wives—an overview." Monthly Labor Review 99 (May): 12–19.

Hedges, J. N. and J. K. Barnett
1972   "Working women and the division of household tasks." Monthly Labor Review (April): 9–14.

Herzog, E. and C. E. Sudia
1973   "Children in fatherless families." In B. M. Caldwell and

H. N. Ricciutti (eds.), Child Development and Social Policy. Chicago: University of Chicago Press.

Hill, Robert B.
1977 Informal Adoption among Black Families. Washington, D.C.: National Urban League.

Hoffman, Saul
1977 "Marital instability and the economic status of women." Demography 14 (February): 67–76.
1979 "Black–white life cycle earnings differences and the vintage hypothesis: a longitudinal analysis." American Economic Review 69 (December): 855–867.

Hoffman, Saul and John Holmes
1976 "Husbands, wives, and divorce." Pp. 23–76 in G. Duncan and J. Morgan (eds.), Five Thousand American Families— Patterns of Economic Progress. Vol. 4. Ann Arbor: Institute for Social Research, University of Michigan.

Horowitz, Ann
1974a "The patterns and causes of changes in white–nonwhite income differences, 1947–72." In G. M. Von Furstenberg et al. (eds.), Patterns of Racial Discrimination. Vol. 2: Employment and Income. Lexington, Mass.: D. C. Heath.
1974b "Trends in the distribution of family income within and between racial groups." In C. M. Von Furstenberg et al. (eds.), Patterns of Racial Discrimination. Vol. 2: Employment and Income. Lexington, Mass.: D. C. Heath.

Hoyak, E. E.
1966 "White–nonwhite differentials: overview and implications." Demography 3 (November): 548–565.

Hutchins, Robert M.
1979 "Welfare, remarriage, and marital search." American Economic Review 69 (June): 369–379.

Iams, Howard M. and Arland Thornton
1975 "Decomposition of differences: a cautionary note." Sociological Methods and Research 3 (February): 341–352.

Jackson, Jacqueline
1971 "But where are the men?" Black Scholar 3 (December): 30–41.

Jaffe, A. J.
1975 "Comments on V. K. Oppenheimer's 'The Life Cycle Squeeze: The Interaction of Men's Occupational and Family Life Cycles'." Demography 12 (May): 331–342.

Janowitz, B.
1973   "The effect of demographic factors on age composition and the implications for per capita income." Demography 10: 507–515.

Johnson, Beverly L.
1978   "Women who head families: their numbers rise, income lags." Monthly Labor Review 101 (February): 32–37.

Kain, John F.
1968   "The distribution and movement of jobs and industry." In J. Q. Wilson (ed.), The Metropolitan Enigma. Cambridge: Harvard University Press.

Keniston, K. and the Carnegie Council on Children
1977   All Our Children: The American Family under Pressure. New York: Harcourt Brace Jovanovich.

Kitagawa, E.
1955   "Components of a difference between two rates." Journal of the American Statistical Association 1 (December): 68–74.
1964   "Standardized comparisons in population research." Demography 1: 296–315.

Kobrin, Frances E.
1973   "Household headship and its changes in the United States, 1940–1960, 1970." Journal of the American Statistical Association 68 (December): 793–800.
1976   "The fall of household size and the rise of the primary individual in the U.S." Demography 13 (February): 127–138.

Kreps, Juanita
1971   Sex in the Market Place: American Women at Work. Baltimore: Johns Hopkins University Press.

Layard, Richard and Antoni Zabalza
1979   "Family income distribution: explanation and policy evaluation." Journal of Political Economy 87 (October): S133–S162.

Lazear, E. P. and R. T. Michael
1980   "Family size and the distribution of real per capita income." American Economic Review 70 (March): 91–107.

Lerner, Greda (ed.)
1973   Black Women in White America. New York: Vintage Books.

Levinger, G. and O. C. Moles (eds.)
1979   Divorce and Separation. New York: Basic Books.

Levitan, Sar and Robert Taggart III
  1974   Employment and Earnings Inadequacy: A New Social Indica-
          tor. Baltimore: Johns Hopkins University Press.
Levitan, S. A., W. B. Johnston, and R. Taggart
  1975   Still a Dream. Cambridge: Harvard University Press.
Levy, F.
  1978   "The harried staffer's guide to current welfare reform pro-
          posals." Welfare Reform Policy Analysis Series, No. 4. Wash-
          ington, D.C.: The Urban Institute.
Lieberson, S. and F. Fugitt
  1967   "Negro–white occupational differences in the absence of dis-
          crimination." American Journal of Sociology 73 (September):
          188–200.
Liebow, Elliot
  1967   Tally's Corner: A Study of Negro Streetcorner Men. Boston:
          Little, Brown & Co.
Liebowitz, Arleen
  1974   "Home investments in children." Journal of Political Economy
          82 (March/April): 111–131.
Lloyd, Cynthia B. (ed.)
  1975   Sex, Discrimination, and the Division of Labor. New York:
          Columbia University Press.
Longfellow, C.
  1979   "Divorce in context: Its impact on children." In G. Levinger
          and O. C. Moles (eds.), Divorce and Separation. New York:
          Basic Books.
McDonald, G. and F. I. Nye
  1979   Family Policy. Minneapolis, Minn.: National Council on Fam-
          ily Relations.
MacDonald, M. and I. V. Sawhill
  1978   "Welfare policy and the family." Public Policy 26 (Winter):
          89–119.
McEaddy, Beverly Johnson
  1976   "Women who head families: a socioeconomic analysis."
          Monthly Labor Review 99 (June): 3–9.
McGraw, Louise
  1977   "Family budgets." Monthly Labor Review 100 (July): 36–39.
Marshall, Ray
  1974   "The economics of racial discrimination: a survey." Journal of
          Economic Literature 12 (September): 849–871.

Masters, S.
   1975   Black–White Income Differentials. New York: Academic Press.
Miao, Greta
   1974   "Marital instability and unemployment among whites and nonwhites, the Moynihan Report revisited." Journal of Marriage and the Family 36: 77–86.
Michael, R. T., V. R. Fuchs and S. R. Scott
   1980   "Changes in the propensity to live alone: 1950–76." Demography 17 (February): 39–56.
Mincer, Jacob
   1976   Schooling and Earnings. New York: National Bureau of Economic Research.
Mincer, Jacob and S. Polachek
   1974   "Family investments in human capital: earnings of women." Journal of Political Economy 82 (May/June): 76–109.
Moon, Marilyn
   1977   The Measurement of Economic Welfare: Its Application to the Aged Poor. New York: Academic Press.
Moon, Marilyn and Eugene Smolensky
   1977   Improving Measures of Economic Well-Being. New York: Academic Press.
Moore, K. A. and S. B. Caldwell
   1976   "Out-of-wedlock pregnancy and childbearing." Urban Institute Working Paper 992–02. Washington, D.C.: The Urban Institute.
Morgan, J.
   1972   A Panel Study of Income Dynamics: Study Design, Procedures, Available Data. Ann Arbor: Institute for Social Research, University of Michigan.
   1974a "Changes in global measures." In J. Morgan (ed.), Five Thousand American Families—Patterns of Economic Progress. Vol. 1. Ann Arbor: Institute for Social Research, University of Michigan.
   1976   A Panel Study of Income Dynamics: Procedures and Tape Codes, 1976 Interviewing Year. Ann Arbor: Institute for Social Research, University of Michigan.
   1978   "Intra-family transfers revisited: the support of dependents inside the family." In G. Duncan and J. Morgan (eds.), Five

Thousand American Families—Patterns of Economic Progress. Vol. 6.

Morgan, J. (ed.)
1974b Five Thousand American Families—Patterns of Economic
Progress. Vols. 1–2. Ann Arbor: Institute for Social Research,
University of Michigan.

Moynihan, Daniel P.
1965 The Negro Family: The Case for National Action. Washington, D.C.: U.S. Government Printing Office.
1973 The Politics of a Guaranteed Income: The Nixon Administration and the Family Assistance Plan. New York: Random
House.

Norton, A. J. and P. C. Glick
1979 "Marital instability in America: Past, present, and future."
Pp. 6–19 in G. Levinger and O. C. Moles (eds.), Divorce and
Separation. New York: Basic Books.

O'Connor, James F.
1977 "A logarithmic technique for decomposing change." Sociological Methods and Research 6 (August): 91–102.

Oppenheimer, V. K.
1970 The Female Labor Force in the United States: Demographic
and Economic Factors Governing Its Growth and Changing
Composition. Population Monograph Series, No. 5. West-
port, Conn.: Greenwood Press.
1974 "The life-cycle squeeze: the interaction of men's occupational
and family cycles." Demography 11 (May): 227–245.
1976 "The Easterlin hypothesis: another aspect of the echo to consider." Population and Development Review 2 (September):
433–457.
1977 "The sociology of women's economic role in the family."
American Sociological Review 42 (June): 387–406.

Orshansky, Mollie
1965 "Counting the poor: another look at the poverty profile." Social Security Bulletin 28 (January): 3–29.
1968 "The shape of poverty in 1966." Social Security Bulletin 31
(March): 3–32.
1969 "How poverty is measured." Monthly Labor Review 92 (February): 37–41.

Plotnick, R. D. and F. Skidmore
  1975   Progress against Poverty: A Review of the 1964–1974 Decade. New York: Academic Press.
Plotnick, R. D. and T. Smeeding
  1979   "Poverty and income transfers: past trends and future prospects." Public Policy 27 (Summer): 259–272.
Preston, S. H.
  1975   "Estimating the proportion of American marriages that end in divorce." Sociological Methods and Research 3 (May): 435–460.
Preston, S. H. and J. McDonald
  1979   "The incidence of divorce within cohorts of American marriages contracted since the Civil War." Demography 16 (February): 1–25.
Preston, S. H. and A. T. Richards
  1975   "The influence of women's work opportunities on marriage rates." Demography 12 (May): 209–222.
Rainwater, L. and W. L. Yancey
  1967   The Moynihan Report and the Politics of Controversy. Cambridge: M.I.T. Press.
Rice, R. M.
  1977   American Family Policy. New York: Family Service Association of America.
Robinson, John P.
  1977   How Americans Use Time: A Social-Psychological Analysis of Everyday Behavior. New York: Praeger.
Ross, H. and I. Sawhill
  1975   Time of Transition: The Growth of Families Headed by Women. Washington, D.C.: The Urban Institute.
Sawhill, I., G. E. Peabody, C. A. Jones, and S. B. Caldwell
  1975   "Income Transfers and Family Structure." Urban Institute Paper 979–03. Washington, D.C.: The Urban Institute.
Scanzoni, J.
  1977   The Black Family in Modern Society. Chicago: University of Chicago Press.
Schultz, T. (ed.)
  1974   Economics of the Family. Chicago: University of Chicago Press.

Siegel, Paul
   1965   "On the cost of being a Negro." Sociological Inquiry 35 (Winter): 41–57.
Slater, C. M.
   1980   "Pieces of the Puzzle." American Demographics 2 (February): 24–27.
Smeeding, Timothy M.
   1977   "The economic well-being of low-income households: implications for income inequality and poverty." Chapter 8 in M. Moon and E. Smolensky (eds.), Improving Measures of Economic Well-Being. New York: Academic Press.
Smith, James P.
   1979   "The distribution of family earnings." Journal of Political Economy 87 (October): S163–S192.
Smith, James P. and Finis Welch
   1978   "Race differences in earnings: a survey and new evidence." Santa Monica, Calif.: Rand Corporation R–2295–NSF.
Smolensky, E. et al.
   1977   "In-kind transfers and the size distribution of income." Chapter 7 in M. Moon and E. Smolensky (eds.), Improving Measures of Economic Well-Being. New York: Academic Press.
Snyder, D. and P. Hudis
   1976   "Occupational income and the effects of minority competition and segregation: a reanalysis and some new evidence." American Sociological Review 41 (April): 209–234.
Spanier, G. and P. Glick
   1980   "Mate selection differentials between whites and blacks in the United States." Social Forces 58 (March): 707–725.
Stack, Carol
   1974   All Our Kin: Strategies for Survival in a Black Community. New York: Harper and Row.
Stafford, Frank and Greg Duncan
   1977   "The use of time and technology by households in the United States." Unpublished paper.
Stolzenberg, Ross M.
   1973   Occupational Difference in Wage Discrimination against Black Men. Ph.D. dissertation, University of Michigan.
   1974   "Estimating an equation with multiplicative and additive terms, with an application to wage differentials between men

and women in 1960." Sociological Methods and Research 2 (February): 313–331.

1975a   "Occupation, education, and wage differentials between white and black men." American Journal of Sociology 81 (September): 299–324.

1975b   "Occupation, markets, and wages." American Sociological Review 40 (October): 645–665.

Sulvetta, M. B.

1978   "The impact of welfare reform on benefits for the poor." Welfare Reform Policy Analysis Series, No. 3. Washington, D.C.: The Urban Institute.

Suter, Larry and Herman Miller

1973   "Income differences between men and career women." American Journal of Sociology 78 (January): 962–974.

Sweet, J. A.

1971   "The employment of wives and inequality of family income." Pp. 1–5 in Proceedings of the Social Statistics Section. Washington, D.C.: American Statistical Association.

1972   "The living arrangements of separated, widowed, and divorced mothers." Demography 9 (February): 143–157.

1973   Women in the Labor Force. New York: Seminar Press.

1975   "Recent trends in the employment of American women." Working Paper 75–14. Madison: Center for Demography and Ecology, University of Wisconsin.

1978   "Recent trends in the household and family status of young adults." Working Paper 78–9. Madison: Center for Demography and Ecology, University of Wisconsin.

Thompson, Gayle B.

1979   "Black–white differences in private pensions: findings from the retirement history study." Social Security Bulletin 42 (February): 15–22.

1978   "Pension coverage and benefits, 1972: findings from the retirement history study." Social Security Bulletin 42 (February): 3–17.

Thurow, L.

1969   Poverty and Discrimination. Washington, D.C.: The Brookings Institute.

Treas, J. and R. Walther

1978a   "Family structure and the distribution of family income." Social Forces 56 (March): 866–880.

1978b   "Households, family structure, and the racial distribution of income, 1968–75." Paper presented at the annual meeting of the Population Association of America, Atlanta (April).

Treiman, D. and K. Terrell

1975a   "Sex and the process of status attainment: a comparison of working women and men." American Sociological Review 40 (April): 174–200.

1975b   "Women, work, and wages—trends in the female occupational structure." In Kenneth Land and Seymour Spilerman (eds.), Social Indicator Models. New York: Russell Sage.

U.S. Bureau of the Census

1960   Census of Population. Vol. 1 and Subject Reports PC(2)–4A, 4B, 4C, 4E, 6A.

1969   Current Population Report, P–23, No. 28.

1970a   Census of the Population. Vol. 1 and Subject Reports PC(2)– 4A, 4B, 4C, 4D, 4E, 5A–5C, 6A–6E, 7A–7F, 8A–8C, 9A, 9B.

1970b   Current Population Report, P–20, No. 212.

1970c   Current Population Report, P–60, No. 75.

1970d   Current Population Report, P–60, No. 76.

1972   A Public Use Sample of Basic Records from the 1970 Census: Description and Technical Documentation.

1974a   Current Population Report, P–23, No. 50.

1974b   Current Population Report, P–23, No. 54.

1975a   Current Population Report, P–20, No. 287.

1975b   Current Population Report, P–20, No. 291.

1975c   Current Population Report, P–20, No. 292.

1975d   Current Population Report, P–20, No. 295.

1975e   Current Population Report, P–20, No. 297.

1975f   Current Population Report, P–20, No. 301.

1975g   Current Population Report, P–23, No. 52.

1975h   Current Population Report, P–23, No. 58.

1975i   A Public Use Sample of Basic Records from the 1960 Census: Description and Technical Documentation.

1976a   Current Population Report, P–20, No. 296.

1976b   Current Population Report, P–20, No. 306.

1976c   Current Population Report, P–23, No. 63.

1976d   Current Population Report, P–60, No. 103.

1977a   1976 March Annual Demographic Microdata File: Technical Documentation.

1977b   Current Population Report, P–20, No. 311.

1977c Current Population Report, P–60, No. 104.

1977d Current Population Report, P–60, No. 105.

1977e Current Population Report, P–60, No. 106.

1978   Current Population Report, P–23, No. 66.

1979   Current Population Report, P–60, No. 119.

U.S. Congress, Congressional Budget Office

1977   "Poverty status of families under alternative definitions of in-come." Background Paper No. 17. Washington, D.C.: U.S. Government Printing Office (June).

U.S. Department of Agriculture

1967   Family Economic Review. Washington, D.C.: U.S. Government Printing Office.

U.S. Department of Health, Education, and Welfare

1976   The Measure of Poverty. Technical Papers. Vol. 1–10. Washington, D.C.: U.S. Government Printing Office. (Especially Technical Paper 1: Documentation of Background Information and Rationale for Current Poverty Matrix, Technical Paper 3: A Review of the Definition and Measurement of Poverty.)

U.S. Department of Health, Education, and Welfare, Social Security Administration

1979   "Men and women: changing roles and Social Security." Social Security Bulletin 42 (May): 25–32.

U.S. Department of Labor, Bureau of Labor Statistics

1968   Revised Equivalence Scale for Estimating Incomes or Budget Costs by Family Types. Bulletin No. 1570–2.

1969   Three Standards of Living for an Urban Family of Four Persons: Spring, 1967. Bulletin No. 1580–5.

1975   Manpower Report of the President.

1976a Employment and Earnings. Vol. 22.

1976b Revised Equivalence Scale for Estimating Income and Budget Costs by Family Type.

Vanek, Joann

1974   "Time spent on housework." Scientific American (November): 116–120.

Vickery, Clair

1977   "The time-poor: a new look at poverty." Journal of Human Resources 12 (Winter): 27–48.

Waite, Linda

1976   "Working wives: 1940–60." American Sociological Review 41 (February): 65–79.

Waldman, E.
   1970   "Women at work: changes in the labor force activity of wom-
          en." Monthly Labor Review (June): 10–18.
Waldman, E., A. S. Grossman, H. Hayghe, and B. L. Johnson
   1979   "Working mothers in the 1970s: a look at the statistics."
          Monthly Labor Review 102 (October): 39–49.
Wargon, S.
   1974   "The study of household and family units in demography."
          Journal of Marriage and the Family 36 (August): 560.
Watts, Harold W.
   1969   "An economic definition of poverty." Pp. 322–325 in D. P.
          Moynihan (ed.), On Understanding Poverty. New York: Basic
          Books.
Weed, J.
   1978   "Trends in marital disruption: implications for health needs
          assessment." Paper presented at the annual meeting of the
          American Sociological Association, San Francisco (Sep-
          tember).
Weisskoff, Francine Blau
   1972   " 'Women's place' in the labor market." American Economic
          Review, Papers and Proceedings. 62 (May): 161–166.
Welch, Finis
   1973   "Black–white differences in returns to schooling." American
          Economic Review 63 (December): 893–907.
Westcott, Diane
   1976   "Youth in the labor force: an area study." Monthly Labor Re-
          view 99 (July): 3–9.
Winsborough, H. H. and Peter Dickinson
   1971   "Components of negro–white income differences." Proceed-
          ings of the Social Statistics Section, American Statistical Asso-
          ciation (August): 6–8.
Wohlstetter, Albert and Sinclair Coleman
   1972   "Race differences in income." In. A. Pascal (ed.), Racial Dis-
          crimination in Economic Life. Lexington, Mass.: D. C. Heath.
Zimbalist, S. E.
   1977   "Replacing our obsolete poverty line." Unpublished manu-
          script.

Index

Affirmative action, 143–144
Age
  adjustment, poverty levels
    and, 152, 154
  children's
    female employment and, 73,
      80, 81, 84
    housework, child care time
      and, 156
    female householder's employ-
      ment, 69, 73, 80, 84
    at first marriage, 30, 144
    male employment and, 69, 88
    need measure construction
      and, 158, 159
Age–sex differentials, 22
Aid to Families with Dependent
  Children (AFDC), 139
  income levels, divorce and,
    39–40, 41
Althauser, Robert, 105

Bane, M. J., 140, 144
Births, out-of-wedlock, 3, 30, 36,
  39, 42. *See also* Fertility
Blacks
  capital gains and profits in in-
    come of, 15–16
  children of

Blacks (*continued*)
  in female-head families,
    35–36
  living with parents, 46–47
  "doubling up" of households
    by, 42
  earning inequalities and, 105,
    109–110
  economic well-being of
    (white–black differences
    in), 112–134
  family income deterioration
    and, 113
  female earnings and, 59–65, 99
  female-head employment and,
    73–80, 81, 84, 85–87
  female-head households and,
    3, 35–37
  household headship and,
    10–11, 12
  husband–wife earnings and,
    54–58
  husband–wife households of,
    progress and, 136
  income sources of, 48–54
  individual vs. family income
    improvement and, 3
  "informal adoption" of chil-
    dren and, 43–46